PREACHING TO
SUFFERERS

PREACHING TO SUFFERERS

GOD AND THE PROBLEM OF PAIN

KENT D. RICHMOND

ABINGDON PRESS

Nashville

This book is printed on acid-free paper.

Library of Congress Cataloging-in-Publication Data

Richmond, Kent D., 1939–
   Preaching to sufferers: God and the problem of pain / Kent D.
Richmond.
       p.   cm.
   Bibliography: p.
   Includes index.
   ISBN 0-687-33873-5 (alk. paper)
   1. Theodicy. 2. Suffering—Religious aspects—Christianity.
3. Preaching. I. Title.
BT160.R53 1988
231'.8—dc19   88-6510
                                                                            CIP

Scripture quotations in this publication, unless otherwise noted are from the
Revised Standard Version of the Bible, copyrighted 1946, 1952, © 1971, 1973
by the Division of Christian Education of the National Council of the
Churches of Christ in the U.S.A., and are used by permission.

Scripture quotations noted KJV are from the King James Version of the Bible.

Excerpts from *J. B.: A Play in Verse* by Archibald MacLeish. Copyright © 1956,
1957, 1958 by Archibald MacLeish. Copyright © renewed 1986 by William H.
MacLeish and Mary H. Grimm. Reprinted by permission of Houghton
Mifflin Company

Excerpts from *Encountering Evil*, ed. by Stephen T. Davis, © 1981 by John
Knox Press. Used by permission.

Manufactured by the Parthenon Press at
Nashville, Tennessee, United States of America

To the memory of
Kent Stephen,
whose short life taught us
much about suffering; and
to Dorothy, Tim, and Steve:
partners in ministry.

Contents

Preface.. 9

Introduction...13

Chapter One - The Nature of the Problem.................. 19

Chapter Two - Answers That Do Not........................36

    Suffering: A Mystery.. 37

    Suffering: A Product of Dualism............................39

    Suffering: A Help in Perceiving Goodness................ 43

    Suffering: A Punishment for Sin............................46

    Suffering: From the Misuse of Human Freedom........ 49

    Suffering: A Means of Testing................................52

Chapter Three - A Two-story Universe......................59

    A Different Understanding of Omnipotence..............60

    The Process Approach... 62

Chapter Four - The Pastor's Own Vulnerability..........79

    Dealing with the Feelings.....................................80

    Pastoral Vulnerability... 89

    Use and Misuse of Prayer.................................... 91

Chapter Five - Light in the Presence of Darkness........ 99

    Allowing the Questions to Speak......................... 103

    The Inevitability of Death................................... 108

The Importance of Each Day....................................111
Speaking of God..112
The Need for Meaning..116
Two Uniquely Painful Experiences.........................119
Afterword..128
Appendix A - Scripture Resources..........................132
Appendix B - Sample Sermons...............................134
Selected Bibliography...152
Index of Scripture References.................................159
Index of Authors..160

Preface

Countless people have confronted the mystery of theodicy or, as it is more popularly known, the problem of pain. Not all of them choose to make that experience the beginning of a process of research culminating in a manuscript. That I have chosen to do so is not so much the result of a belief that the loss of our first son in any way makes me unique, but rather because I have learned so much as a result of young Kent's death. What I have learned has provided the foundation for an ability to share similar experiences with bereaved persons over a ministry of more than twenty years. It is my hope that this experience, coupled with the result of research, will prove to be of help to other pastors and laypersons who confront the problem of suffering in their lives and ministries.

I have many people to thank for help given directly and indirectly toward the preparation of this volume. The Wisconsin Conference of The United Methodist Church and its United Methodist Foundation support a program that allows pastors to spend time away from the pressure of the parish for the purpose of study. The members of my parish at the time, the Asbury United Methodist Church of La Crosse, Wisconsin, carried on in my absence. They were assisted in this regard by Lee C. and Betty Moorehead, who delayed their retirement to provide pastoral care to the congregation. They are remembered with warmth.

The library staff at Garrett-Evangelical Theological Seminary took this computer neophyte under their "wing" and oriented him in the use of the computer, which now controls the filing. Without their help, I would have had a great deal of difficulty locating materials.

There is no way to express adequately my appreciation to my mentors, but to the late George A. Buttrick and to Merrill Abbey and Donald Chatfield must go my deep thanks. It was they who taught me to love and respect the homiletical art. Merrill and Don also gave their time to read the first manuscript of this volume. All have been pastors and friends to me and to my family.

The manuscript rewrite came during the time of my clinical residency at the Mayo Medical Center—Rochester Methodist Hospital. I have appreciated the opportunity to test my feelings about hospital ministry in such an intense setting. It would be impossible to remember all of the staff persons, patients, and other persons who were a part of that learning experience, but special thanks should go to the members of the pastoral care staff and to the nurses of Station 11-1, Respiratory Intensive Care. It was my good fortune to spend most of my clinical residency working with those nurses. They are a real example of grace under pressure.

I am also indebted to my Rochester host, Thomas Tempero, who opened his home and his fellowship to me.

My parents, Kenneth and Harriet Richmond, and my wife's parents, Raymond and Thyra Johnson, shared the pain of losing a grandchild, but gave to us the generational assurance that the best was yet to come.

I would also take this opportunity to extend a special word of respect and affection to my brother Terry. He has also been to "the valley of the shadow" and has returned stronger. No elder brother could have a more deeply caring younger brother.

Finally, to my wife, Dorothy, who has been my partner and friend for the last twenty-five years, and to our sons, Timothy and Stephen, who so fill my world with joy, this volume is yours as well, for your love has made it all worthwhile!

Rochester, Minnesota
Pentecost, 1987

Introduction

His name was Kent. His birth, over twenty years ago, was the culmination of the hopes and dreams of his mother and father. It was an occasion of great rejoicing. He was born full-term; the delivery was completely normal. One week later, he died. Some unexplained malady, frustrating all of the efforts of those who tried to save him, carried him away from the sound of his parents' voices, put him out of reach of the parents who wanted to hold and to love him. He was our firstborn, and his death devastated me and my wife.

Kent's death was our first experience with what in the theological world is referred to as the problem of *theodicy*. It is known to more of us as the problem of suffering, or the problem of evil.

In some cases, being able to label a problem or an event makes it easier to understand. That is not the case with the suffering or death of someone deeply loved. Knowing the name does nothing to alleviate the pain, the intense frustration, the deep disbelief.

Friends came to call, fulfilling the church's mission

to surround the bereaved with a community of love. Their support was deeply appreciated, but there was no way in which the friends could feel the loss at the same level we did. Only those whose lives had been touched by the same mystery knew what we were feeling. They were able to touch our pain in a more meaningful way. They had been to "the valley of the shadow." They understood.

It is now twenty years later, and I have joined the ranks of those who understood. My wife's and my experience with the death of a child has been repeated many times in the lives of those families with whom I have ministered in four congregations. I would never have guessed at the time of our son's death that the experience would enable me to better empathize with persons going through a similar experience, but that has been the case. Someone of a skeptical bent might suggest that there ought to be better means for discovering how grief feels; true though that may be, it changes nothing. Dag Hammarskjöld said it better: "We are not permitted to choose the frame of our destiny. But what we put into it is ours."[1]

I have chosen to put my experience with the problem of pain into a ministry with other persons. I have wrestled with that mystery over the intervening years. I have read and researched, written and preached about suffering to the point where, for my own life at least, I have been enabled to come to terms with suffering. In a very real sense, however, no one ever comes to terms with suffering. Answers and pseudo-answers abound for the mystery of innocent suffering. I know of none of them that adequately and fully speaks to all of the ins and outs of the problem. Some approaches are more helpful than others. They provide opportunities for the pastor to offer a greater measure of hope to those who stand bereft in the face of the mystery. More than that, they offer a means of holding onto faith in God at the same time that one is aware only of the pain of loss. In this volume, these approaches to the problem of pain will be explored.

A few words are necessary at the beginning with regard to the scope of the journey upon which we are about to embark. In no sense is this volume an exhaustive treatment of all of the approaches to the problem of theodicy. That is the task of the theologian or the philosopher, and helpful studies that cover the ground are available.[2] Nevertheless, I have attempted to illustrate the inadequacies of some approaches to suffering, and at the same time I have lifted up others for consideration as helpful alternatives. What is of help, of course, is a purely subjective affair and has much to do with one's theological stance. The approaches I have found helpful are those that have brought hope to families to whom I have ministered through the pain and bereavement. It is my hope that these approaches will provide opportunities for ministry for others as well. One approach in particular, that of the God who stands with us in suffering, seems to me to offer the most hope and consolation to those journeying through the difficult days of pain.

The volume concludes by looking at the ultimate question: When the problem of suffering finds its end in the death of someone we love, what then can be said? I believe that there are yet words that can be spoken, words that may bring consolation and promise to the pain of those who grieve. Accordingly, the volume's

15

final emphasis is on themes that can and have been helpfully preached at such times. These themes are further illustrated in the sample sermons that comprise Appendix B. It is my hope that these resources will be of help to pastors and seminary students as they minister to those who mourn.

Unless seminary curricula have changed considerably in recent years, the funeral service—the spoken word, the rituals, the symbols—still seems to be the act of ministry for which pastors receive the least amount of training. Many of us can remember the first time we were called upon to be with a family during a time of intense grief and the frustration we felt at not knowing what to do or say. I hope that this volume will offer some help in that regard.

Nickles, the character who represents Satan in Archibald MacLeish's play *J.B.*, makes the statement that is also very present in the minds of those who suffer. Without a trace of doubt, he affirms:

> If God is God He is not good,
> If God is good He is not God.[3]

That is the charge with which we must contend in the chapters to come.

Notes

1. Dag Hammarskjöld, *Markings*, foreword by W. H. Auden (New York: Alfred A. Knopf, 1964), p. 55.

2. See, for example, S. Paul Schilling, *God and Human Anguish* (Nashville: Abingdon Press, 1977).

3. Archibald MacLeish, *J.B.* (Cambridge, Mass.: Houghton Mifflin, 1986), p. 11.

Chapter One
The Nature of the Problem

Millions and millions of mankind
Burned, crushed, broken mutilated,
Slaughtered, and for what? For thinking!
For walking round the world in the wrong
Skin, the wrong-shaped noses, eyelids:
Sleeping the wrong night wrong city—
London, Dresden, Hiroshima.
There never could have been so many
Suffered more for less."

Nickles, in *J.B.*

Atheism arises out of human suffering. . . .
Dorothee Soelle, *Suffering*

Her name was Kris. It was evident from the moment she entered the world that, unlike some other children, she was not well. A beautiful child, she was born with a rare disease that caused her outer skin to slough off, leaving the inner muscle tissue exposed. The physicians described her condition as a "one-in-ten-million" occurrence, noted that there was no cure, and informed her parents that she could not be expected to live long. They had not, however, counted on Kris' extraordinary desire to live. She went on, day after day, week after week. Each day, the dressings needed to be changed over the exposed muscle tissue, a painful process for her that tore at the emotions of her parents and robbed Kris of her badly needed strength. Eventually, as one organ after another shut down, some three months after birth, she died. She left all those near to her asking, *Why?* Why was she born with the disease? Where was God when her parents lifted their prayers for healing? What kind of God allows a beautiful child to suffer as Kris did?

These questions are typical. They are at the heart of the problem of pain. They provide part of the moving force behind our human desire to struggle with the problem of suffering in search of understanding. The questions are at least as old as faith itself. With every decision to believe in God comes also an expectation that making the leap of faith will result in a better life for those who make the commitment. Reinhold Niebuhr was not the first to note that the "natural instincts of religion demand that my life be given meaning by a special security against all the insecurities of life."[1] Indeed, as one watches the slick, professional presentation of Christianity on much of today's religious television, one is struck by how deeply imbedded is the notion that faith in Christ will somehow protect one from the vicissitudes of life. One searches these programs in vain for a vision of the lame, the halt, and the blind. It is no wonder, then, that the pastor is confronted with astonishment on the part of the faithful when they discover that the Gospel writer believed that the "Father who is in heaven . . . sends rain on the just and on the unjust" (Matt. 5:45) alike.

If pastors have not wrestled with the problem of evil somewhere in the course of a seminary career, the first encounter with it in the life of a parish family will soon drive them back to the books in search of a way to explain the unexplainable. If pastors pursue the quest, they will soon learn that volumes have been written on the subject of theodicy. So much has been written that some feel that "one of the clearest signs of divine restraint, of God's will to let [the] creation be . . . is the continuing existence of theologians . . . not least of all theologians functioning as ever-so-well-meaning theo-dicists."[2] Others, such as Sam Keen, feel that "all attempts to rationalize or explain evil . . . must be abandoned," since such efforts tend to lull people into the "illusion that evil is somehow confined, limited, and conquered in principle if not in fact."[3]

There is no doubt that avoiding the attempt to deal with the problem of pain would be easier than the intellectual wrestling that the problem requires of those who pursue it, but such avoidance does little to help the earnest pastor who wants to be able to speak meaningfully to families in the parish whose lives have been broken apart by the mystery. Neither is such avoidance faithful to the gospel's mandate to us to preach the Word, which can bring wholeness and healing to battered spirits. When a mother, facing the death of her child, asks why, the pastor must be able to do more than shrug the shoulders and imply that such questions are better left unasked.

The problem of evil is an issue to pastors in two

21

particular ways. They encounter it in their own lives, in the threatening Xray that suggests a promising career might come to an early end. They encounter it also in the lives of those to whom they minister each day, who ask the question: "Why me?"

In our psychological age, the tendency is to explore scientific answers.

> One can discuss what is known of the causes of cancer and seek to understand how they have operated in this case. I for one believe that this kind of explanation has an important role to play, that many of us benefit emotionally and spiritually, as well as intellectually, from knowing what is going on, evil though it may be. But this is not the kind of answer for which the parishioner turns to the pastor.[4]

Pastors are not being asked to play amateur physician or therapist. They are being asked to speak out of their own specialty, the realm of faith. If pastors are not able to answer persons' questions with finality, they must at least be able to provide a means by which persons can come to think about an illness and place it into an understanding of life and death, illuminated by the gospel of Christ. To do any less is "to fail to take the questioner with full seriousness as a human being,"[5] as a child of God. More than that, Paul Irion has argued that a person's ability to cope with an illness is directly related to that person's ability to "articulate an understanding of death that is meaningful."[6] To laypersons and clergy alike, it is the word of faith that enables us to continue to hope in the face of suffering.

Not all forms of belief find a thorny problem in the presence of innocent suffering in God's world. A dualistic faith, for example, which posits a good as well as an evil deity, makes ample accommodation for evil and suffering in the action of the evil principle. Christianity, however, by its monotheistic nature, attributes all events in some measure to the influence of God. Moreover, if as Genesis suggests, God looked out over the created world and pronounced it "good," then the problem immediately arises as to the origin of the evil existing in that world.

The problem becomes more acute through the New Testament's affirmation that the nature of the God revealed in Jesus Christ is love. James S. Stewart, whose sermons on the problem of suffering are among the most thoughtful, has noted that "it is precisely our Christian faith that creates the problem. There is no real problem of evil for the man who has never accepted the Christian revelation [for] only the Christian says, 'God is love!'"[7] As we will see further on, one of the approaches to the problem of pain involves the surrender of the traditional notion of God's goodness. For now, however, suffice it to say that Christianity has a problem in attempting to reconcile a God with an inherently loving nature who maintains some sort of control or influence over the created world on the one hand, with the very evident and contradictory existence of evil and suffering present in that world on the other.

The problem was discussed early in the history of Christianity. Augustine, Bishop of Hippo, wrote of it:

> Here is God, and here is what God has created; and God is good and is most mightily and incomparably better than all these. Yet He, being good, created them good. . . . Where, then, is evil? Where did it come from and how did it creep in here? What is its root and seed? (Augustine, *Confessions*, VII, 5)

In other words, if God is good, then why does God allow evil and suffering in the creation? Does God not care about the welfare of the creation? Or is God, perhaps, too busy to be bothered with monitoring the conditions in the created world? If that is so, then the question arises as to whether God can truly be called good. That is the nature of the problem with which we contend. It is a problem that does not yield to easy solutions.

Traditionally, Christians have regarded God as good and omnipotent. Suffering and pain strike at the heart of those concepts. Noting that the presence of evil and suffering are all too evident in the world, the sufferer asks, "Where is God? Does God not hear my prayer for help? Why does God not answer?" If God is good, why is there no response? Annie Dillard wrote that the minister at the church in which she worshiped once paused in the middle of a pastoral prayer of intercession to say, "Lord, we bring you these petitions every week."[8] Those who repeatedly petition God for help in the midst of their suffering can be forgiven for wondering if God is indeed good when there seems so little response to their praying.

Questions may also be raised of the traditional understanding of omnipotence. If we hold to a belief in God's absolute goodness and receive no help in response to our praying, it is but a short step to assume that perhaps God is unable to do anything to alleviate our pain, that God is not in control of the universe, whatever that may mean. Hence we come to Nickles' description out of Archibald MacLeish's drama about Job, *J.B.*

If God is God He is not good,
If God is good He is not God.

Obviously, a distinction needs to be made at this point, for not all encounters with evil and suffering cause us to raise these kinds of questions of our faith in God. When, in his mid-eighties, my grandfather succumbed to the rigors of old age, no questions were raised of God's goodness or omnipotence. He had lived a long and full life. He had left his family blessed by his goodness. His death was accepted in the context of the preacher's belief that there is "a time to be born and a time to die" (Eccles. 3:2a). His death was accepted as a natural part of life.

Neither do I call God to account when, in the act of hanging a picture on the wall, I manage to hit my thumb with the hammer. The language occasioned by the event may possibly raise questions as to the nature of my own faith, but I have no one to blame for the pain but myself.

Similarly, there are experiences of suffering that are brought on by virtue of our relationships with other people. When the marriage of friends ends abruptly in divorce, we suffer with those persons because of our love for them. We recognize their responsibility for the lack of communication that fractured the relationship; we do not ordinarily blame God for the break.

Frequently, we suffer as a result of the sin of other people. When a drunken driver causes the death of a friend, we are filled with a real sense of anguish. We may blame the driver and his or her intoxication; we may blame a society that promotes alcohol consumption; we may blame the bartender who served the alcohol, but we do not ordinarily blame God for the tragedy. We know that, if we suffer from someone's misuse of freedom, we also benefit from the contributions of those who use their freedom to alleviate human suffering. As S. Paul Schilling put it:

> Though our inescapable involvement with all other forms of existence often increases our suffering, our awareness of this involvement draws us closer to other living things and makes us more sensitive to their needs. . . . The sensitive person . . . expresses his identification with others in concrete acts aimed at the reduction of the world's pain.[9]

The very accident that claimed the life of someone we loved may be the catalyst that forces the creation of more stringent laws regarding alcohol consumption, more severe penalties upon those who abuse alcohol. Thus our interdependence seems to be a mixture. It brings us great suffering, but it is also the source of untold goodness.

A similar judgment seems to be in order when we consider so-called "natural" evil, or suffering that comes about as a result of forces that are a part of nature. Tornadoes, hurricanes, fire, and flood take their toll of human life. Yet the same river that, while flooding, washes away homes, provides water vital for our survival. There are those who might call such events "acts of God," but the judgment is mixed. George A. Buttrick noted that while we "have to say that God allows pain from natural evil" we should not say "that he inflicts it."[10] Annie Dillard, on the other hand, whose book *Pilgrim at Tinker Creek* graphically describes the violence that she found in the world of nature around her, notes that it's "a hell of a way to run a railroad" and asks, "Is it a better way to run a universe?"[11]

How do we deal with such questions, particularly when they come from persons to whom we are close, persons with whom we minister in our congregations? One way is to hold fast to a belief that an inscrutable God knows what is best and that if such disasters exist "at the expense of man, too bad. God is eternal, man is not."[12] But how do we square such a cavalier attitude with the New Testament's revelation of a God of love, as seen in the ministry of Jesus Christ?

There are those who, holding to a belief in natural law, simply affirm that such events are explained by the laws that keep the universe on an even keel. If they exist at our expense, that is part of the price we must pay for living in a generally beneficent world. But, as Buttrick has written, to say that is to offer an explanation that is little more than an "insult to human sorrow."[13] It certainly provides nothing in the way of hope or understanding. Some might say that we need to take the long view. Yes, some say, each painful event seems filled with questions, but God sees our suffering in the context of *kairos*, God's time. All things even out at the end. There may be an element of truth in such explanations, but if those who offer them couple the explanations with a belief that God is in some sense the author of our misfortunes, then many must demur. Edmund A. Steimle's advice is apt, for the

long stream of history gives an even more ambiguous answer: the truly great achievements in medical science, and Dachau; the powerful forces for justice and peace, and a napalm bomb burning a Vietnamese village to a crisp; the awesome power of nuclear fission, and what? Nagasaki, or a city glowing with

> light and humming with modern conveniences. Find God in
> the confused and surging tides of history down through the
> ages if you can. I can't. It's a mishmash.[14]

It is almost a commonplace to note that, on virtually any issue, there are two sides to the question. There are those who can look at the devastation of a tornado or a spouse whose body is riddled with the ravages of cancer and say, "Well, it's God's will." There are others, facing the same acts of suffering, who find in them the root of severe doubt. For the first time in their lives, all that they held to be true seems called into question. There are even those who would applaud this questioning, finding it to be a necessary step forward on the path to a stronger faith. Dorothee Soelle, remarking on the disbelief that frequently accompanies human suffering, felt that "the faith that disintegrates in this experience is a theism that has almost nothing to do with Christ" and that "the growing atheism of the masses, despite its banality, is a step forward."[15]

Are there, then, issues aroused by suffering upon which all might unite in their questioning? Probably not, but there are some that seem to draw a greater sense of unanimity. All of them are illustrated in the Bible's classic story of the mystery of suffering, the story of Job.

The author of Job wasted no time getting to the heart of the problem. In the very first verse, Job is described as "blameless and upright." He is "one who fears God and turns away from evil" (Job 1:8). In the mythical conversation between God and Satan, even God notes that "there is none like [Job] on the earth, a blameless and upright man" (Job 1:8). Thus one of the first issues that seems to give rise to questions by many is the fact that faith in God seems not to insulate us from suffering. If it could happen to Job, it could happen to anyone.

We have noted above our deep desire to believe that faith in God will protect us from the vicissitudes of life and the tendency of some segments of Christianity to make such a belief one of the cornerstones of their particular version of the faith. This is a notion that seems deeply a part of our consciousness as Americans, perhaps dating back to the Puritans' belief in the providence of God.[16] From childhood, we have been taught that success comes to those who work hard, love the Lord, and deal compassionately with their neighbors. Certainly, there is no inherent harm to be found in such virtues, except as our acceptance of them makes us self-centered. Every pastor has called in the homes of inactive church members whose belief in the Puritan virtues has led them to feel that they do not need to attend or to support their churches. We are also aware of how disillusioned many such persons can become when they encounter misfortune.

The same sort of process can be illustrated on a national scale. Americans tend to believe their nation to be a "Christian" nation whose actions in the global community manifest the will of God. We, and other nations as well, have baptized our wars with a mantle of holiness, turning them into veritable crusades for righteousness. We do not wage war against other nations so much as we contend against a "godless" enemy. Disillusionment came on a national level with the war in Vietnam. The nation with a faith in God did not prevail, and the Vietnamese debacle remains festering on the conscience of many Christians. It goes without saying that such a distorted belief in the providence of God is extremely dangerous in a time of nuclear cold war.[17] A reading of the book of Job will quickly disabuse us of the notion that faith in God protects those who believe.

Closely related to this is the second issue, the notion that those who live righteously, who are not given over to self-centeredness, should experience a life free from suffering. We find no evidence of self-righteousness on Job's part. His devotion was carried even to the extreme of making an offering to God just in case some sin had been committed by someone in his family and had escaped his notice (Job 1:5). How unjust, then, the misfortune that was brought upon him by the deal cut by God with Satan!

Again, however, we need not rely on Job for an illustration of the belief that those who live righteously should somehow be protected from suffering. Yale theologian Henri Nouwen described his own pain as he witnessed the death of his mother.

> The struggle began. We were not prepared for it; we had never even thought about her death as a death with a struggle. We had not anticipated anxiety, fear, and agony. Why should we? Hers was a beautiful, gentle, generous life, marked by giving all there was to give. It could not possibly end in a restless, painful, torturous struggle. Peaceful people should die a peaceful death; faithful people should die a quiet death; loving people should die a gentle death.[18]

When such suffering comes to those we have loved and whom we know have spent their lives giving themselves for others, it is natural for us to raise questions about our faith.

A third issue aroused by suffering, which gives rise to questioning, has to do with presumed innocence on the part of the one who suffers. This is never more true than when the sufferer is an infant or a child. We can readily identify with Job's agony at the loss of his children (1:18ff). Rabbi Harold S. Kushner, whose book *When Bad Things Happen to Good People* became a national best-seller, speaks for many who have experienced the suffering or death of a child. On "what grounds," he asked, did his son "have to suffer? He was an innocent child, a happy, outgoing three-year-old. Why should he have to suffer physical and psychological pain every day of his life?"[19]

If a person suffers a painful death at the conclusion of what seems to have been a particularly evil life, that death may become easier for some to accept. There can even be found those who would tactlessly suggest that such pain is the way God punishes those who have lived badly. We will speak to that issue in time, but for now it is enough to say that the greater degree of presumed innocence on the part of the suffering person, the more difficulty we have in accepting the pain.

A fourth issue that seems to arouse questioning on the part of many has to do with the relative degree of meaninglessness of the suffering taking place. This issue is most often troublesome for those whose faith leads them to feel that most instances of suffering contain a purpose or meaning. It is not uncommon to hear it said that "God is trying to teach me something through my suffering." But when the suffering becomes so intense, its quantity so great, that it seems no longer to serve any conceivable purpose, then faith

31

in a God of love and omnipotence often "has to waver or be destroyed."[20] I recall a friend who was suffering through the last stages of an inoperable cancer. When the pain began, she believed that it was a means by which she was being called to demonstrate her faith through her endurance. But when the intense irritation of a bad case of shingles was added to the pain of cancer, no longer was she able to hold to her belief that a purpose was to be found in the pain. It had become too much.

When one looks at the story of Job and the steadily progressing suffering that he experienced, one finds that the degree of suffering went well beyond any purpose that might have been served through the mythical pact between God and Satan. Suffering can become so intense that, rather than enhancing one's witness by courage or endurance, it serves instead to cause the destruction of that faith.

Finally, the random nature of suffering can also cause us to question God's goodness or omnipotence. The question is commonly heard by pastors: "Why do those who are faithful suffer, while someone down the street, who has no faith at all, seems to lead a life of bliss?" It almost looks as though it is the faithful follower who is especially selected to experience anguish. Certainly this seems to be the case in the story of Job.

Moreover, it often seems that particular groups of people, or races, come in for a disproportionate share of pain. When we look at the struggle of black persons in our nation, we find a disproportionate share of suffering. Can anything in history compare to the systematic persecution that has been visited upon the Jews, often by Christians in the name of Christ? When we look at the genocide perpetrated upon the Jews by the Nazis during World War II, we recoil in horror in the face of such bestiality.

It does not help to suggest that the Holocaust was the result of sinful people's exercising their God-given free will. The degree of the pain inflicted and its barbarity are such that we must stand with the death camp prisoner who, watching the hanging of a child, asked in agony, "Where is God?"[21] Actually, such a question seems rather tame compared to the hatred expressed by Berish, the inn-keeper, in Elie Wiesel's play *The Trial of God*.

> If God insists in going on with His methods, let Him—but I won't say Amen. Let Him crush me, I won't say Kaddish. Let Him kill me, let Him kill us all, I shall shout and shout that it's His fault. I'll use my last energy to make my protest known. Whether I live or die, I submit to Him no longer.[22]

In the face of such suffering, then, all of theodicy's painful questions are wrung from the hearts of those who are affected. Try "squaring any of it with an ultimate motive of love,"[23] challenged Paul Scherer, and yet that is the very task that faces us in our congregations almost daily.

In another age, under other circumstances, a king called to the prophet Jeremiah, "Is there any word from the Lord?" (Jer. 27:17). That is still the question on the lips of those who suffer. Can we interpret their suffering and help them understand how suffering can be held in the context of faith in a God of love and omnipotence? It is a responsibility that we cannot evade. There are many interpretations of pain; the time has come to examine some of them.

Notes

1. Ursula M. Niebuhr, ed., *Justice and Mercy* (New York: Harper, 1974), pp. 15-16.

2. David Cain, "A Way of God's Theodicy: Honesty, Presence, Adventure." *The Journal of Pastoral Care* (December 1978): 240.

3. Sam Keen, *Apology for Wonder* (New York: Harper, 1969), p. 107.

4. John B. Cobb, Jr., "The Problem of Evil and the Task of Ministry." In *Encountering Evil*, ed. Stephen T. Davis (Atlanta: John Knox Press, 1981), pp. 167-68. See also Paul Pruyser, *The Minister as Diagnostician* (Philadelphia: Westminster Press, 1976).

5. Ibid., p. 167.

6. Paul E. Irion, "The Agnostic and the Religious: Their Coping with Death." In *Death and Ministry*, eds. Donald J. Bane et al. (New York: Seabury Press, 1975), p. 205.

7. James S. Stewart, *The Strong Name* (New York: Charles Scribner's Sons, 1941), p. 129.

8. Annie Dillard, *Pilgrim at Tinker Creek* (New York: Bantam Books, 1974), p. 58.

9. S. Paul Schilling, *God and Human Anguish* (Nashville: Abingdon Press, 1977), pp. 225-26.

10. George A. Buttrick, *God, Pain, and Evil* (Nashville: Abingdon Press, 1966), pp. 45-46.

11. Dillard, *Pilgrim at Tinker Creek*, p. 179.

12. Elie Wiesel, *The Trial of God*, trans. Marion Wiesel (New York: Random House, 1979), p. 157.

13. Buttrick, *God, Pain, and Evil*, p. 40.

14. Edmund A. Steimle, *God, the Stranger* (Philadelphia: Fortress Press, 1979), pp. 17-23.

15. Dorothee Soelle, *Suffering,* trans. Everett Kalin (Philadelphia: Fortress Press, 1975), pp. 143-44.

16. See, for example, Niebuhr, *Justice and Mercy,* p. 17.

17. Robert Dedmon draws some interesting comparisons between the danger of nuclear war and the book of Job in "Job as Holocaust Survivor." *The St. Luke's Journal of Theology* (June 1983):183-84.

18. Henri J. M. Nouwen, *In Memoriam* (Notre Dame, Ind.: Ave Maria Press, 1980), p. 22.

19. Harold S. Kushner, *When Bad Things Happen to Good People* (New York: Avon Books, 1983), p. 2.

20. Soelle, *Suffering,* p. 142.

21. Elie Wiesel, *Night,* trans. Stella Rodway with a foreword by François Mauriac (New York: Avon Books, 1960), p. *x*.

22. Wiesel, *The Trial of God,* p. 133.

23. Paul Scherer, exposition on the book of Job, in *The Interpreter's Bible,* ed. Nolan B. Harmon, vol. III (New York: Abingdon Press, 1954), p. 1173.

Chapter Two
Answers That Do Not

When tested for finite standards for benevolence, the God of traditional theodicy failed miserably. The strategy devised to protect the ascription of benevolence to God ironically leads to an admission of God's inscrutability. And if God is said to be inscrutably benevolent, has anything of substance been said at all?

Peter I. Kaufman, "Daniel Day Williams and the Science of Suffering"

We say we believe; but when we try to say what we believe, we start handing ourselves a lot of metaphysical scaffolding instead of Jesus. We say we believe in the order of the universe, or in the goodness of God, or in God's plan for the universe. But then a bad day comes along; The universe has no more order than a dump, and God is beating the tar out of us, and his plan looks as if he forgot to make it.

Robert Farrar Capon, *Exit 36*

> *Behold, he will slay me; I have no*
> *   hope;*
> *yet I will defend my ways to his*
> *   face.*

Job 13:15

His name was George. An engaging and attractive young man, he had recently graduated from high school and was spending his summer months working in a scrap yard to help earn enough money to pay for his first year of college. Like many young men, he was enjoying having his first automobile and the freedom of mobility it gave him. From the time he had first put his hands on a steering wheel, he seemed determined to know all he could about the inner workings of a car. He made most repairs himself, as he delighted in breaking down this or that assembly, repairing it, and putting it back together again. His summer job fit right in with that interest. At the scrap yard, he was responsible for salvaging usable parts from junked automobiles.

That's what he was doing on the afternoon he died. Working underneath an automobile and removing the transmission, he was as happy as he could be. Then the chain on the hoist broke, and the car came crashing down on top of him. All of us who knew him were devastated by his death. "How," his parents asked, "could God allow something like that to happen?" Over the course of time, a measure of healing took place in their shattered spirits, though all of us knew that the wound was so deep that it would never heal completely. Looking back at the loss of their son, the parents said eventually, "I guess it's something that we'll never really understand." Their answer represents one of the often-heard attempts to answer the questions raised by the problem of suffering.

SUFFERING: A MYSTERY

There are a great many approaches to the problem of suffering.[1] One of them is that voiced by George's parents. It is possible simply to accept suffering as a mystery, to believe that it is something we will probably never be able to understand. We are left to pick up the pieces of our broken spirits and go on with the business of living. Certainly, there is a long tradition behind this approach to the problem in the history of Christian thought. Job's friend, Bildad, acknowledging the suffering of Job, assured him that

> At the end there will be justice!—
> Justice for All! Justice for everyone!
> On the way—it doesn't matter.[2]

Suffering is a mystery to be accepted.

One of our most popular hymns assures us that "God moves in a mysterious way, His wonders to perform." Lest we continue to fear that all will not be well, the writer goes on to affirm that "God is his own interpreter, and he will make it plain."

Similarly, Paul, no stranger to the problem of suffering, was able to believe that "in everything God works for good with those who love him" (Rom. 8:28). Of course, we must set beside Paul's acceptance of suffering his frequent prayer for the removal of the physical ailment that plagued him, his "thorn in the flesh" (II Cor. 12:7).

The inability to understand the reason for suffering frequently leads persons to dispose of the problem by saying, "Well, it's God's will." When this is said to people who have passed through a time of intense pain, it is not uncommon for them to reply, "Well, if that was God's will, then I want nothing to do with him." There are depths of pain that seem absolutely incompatible with the love of God revealed through Christ. One wants to say, "It's *not* God's will. How can you say such a thing?"

S. Paul Schilling notes several problems inherent in accepting suffering as a mystery. He writes in *God and Human Anguish* that there are those whose "experiences do not enable them to confront bafflement with total trust" in God. Others might well be inclined to view such an approach as little more than an "out of sight, out of mind" brand of thought or, as Schilling puts it, "disposing of the problem by forgetting it." Finally, Schilling found that there is just not enough space in such an approach to accommodate "the operation of other causative agencies,"[3] such as natural disaster or pain brought about by the misuse of human freedom. While the approach may satisfy some, a great many others simply cannot accept it.

SUFFERING: A PRODUCT OF DUALISM

Another common approach to the problem is to regard suffering as the product of an evil principle, a Satan such as is found in the story of Job. In that account, it is Satan who suggests that Job's faithfulness is the product of the blessings showered on his life by God, and it is Satan who suggests that, if God were to remove all of these blessings, Job would "curse thee to thy face" (Job 1:11 KJV).

It is possible to regard this being as the essence of absolute, unadulterated evil. Paul Scherer, however, saw Satan more as

a kind of devil in the making, already more enamored of his faultfinding than is quite decent. He can fairly be seen kicking

39

up the star dust and looking around with a smirk, as if the cynicism he harbors in his heart were a sweet morsel on his tongue.[4]

Whatever the nature of Satan, there is certainly evidence of this belief within the Bible. If we find Satan at work in the Old Testament, we find the concept even more developed in the New. In the Gospels, persons are shown to be under the threat of demon possession. As Jesus brings healing to the sick, it is the demons who are cast out, kicking and screaming their wrath at the God who has disturbed their domination. This is no longer any "devil in the making." The Satan portrayed in Revelation is full-blown evil, clearly ready to do battle to the death against the God whose presence he rejected (see Rev. 20).

The notion that evil and suffering are the work of an evil being or a Satan is not confined to the pages of the Bible; it is very much alive and well in our own day. It can, perhaps, even be said that the notion of demon possession is the only explanation of suffering to enjoy the dubious distinction of having been adopted by the motion picture industry. Beginning, perhaps, with the movie *The Exorcist*, we have witnessed an entire genre of films that have portrayed the activity of demons in the suffering of human beings. Of such films, Steven Spielberg's *Poltergeist* became a box office smash. In that film, a family that seemed at first to be the owners of a house occupied by disturbing, yet relatively harmless, spirits found themselves confronting a terrifying devil at the end.

There are those who, aware of the popularity of these kinds of films, have suggested that demonism has become one of the most popular spiritual beliefs of our day. The late Arthur C. McGill believed that

> every age has a peculiar kind of evil to which it is especially sensitive. . . . Our age seems to be obsessed with the suffering caused by violence. . . . It is felt to be *the scandal* that threatens to undermine all confidence in the decent values that make life possible. For this reason, no literary work or dramatic production, no cowboy television program or profound philosophical novel seems able to claim our serious consideration today unless it stands in relation to an area of violence.[5]

According to McGill, this violence is often caused by something "nonhuman, even though people are involved in it."[6]

Perhaps, in an age that seems so beset by violence, we find it easier to live with ourselves if we can ascribe that violence to the work of an agent outside ourselves. To say, as a popular comedian has, "The devil made me do it!" almost seems to give the violent act a mantle of respectability.

Out of a belief that evil and suffering are acts that break in on our lives through the influence of outside agents (demons), it has become increasingly common to retaliate in kind. The rising incidence of acts of vigilantism reflects the growing frustration of a populace that seems to have grown weary of turning the other cheek. McGill has written, "People today apparently find the most decisive manifestations of power in that which destroys. . . . When men do violence to one another . . . they are exercising a powerfulness that contradicts the power of God."[7] Even more than that, if a person "sees himself in a world where the satanic reigns, then such a person would be insane to act unselfishly."[8]

What are we to make of this? Many of us who received religious training in mainline churches thought we had long ago disposed of the notion of a devil or Satan. Perhaps the lesson to be learned here is that nothing is ever permanently discarded!

There are some very real limitations to a dualistic explanation of the problem of suffering. The most obvious objection comes at the point of belief in the omnipotence of God. If God is indeed all powerful, then why would another power be allowed to wreak so much havoc in the lives of God's children? To answer that question by saying that God will ultimately defeat Satan does nothing to alleviate present pain. Those who suffer now want some sense of understanding now, not a "pie in the sky by and by."

George A. Buttrick recognized that one of the points of appeal to be found in the belief in a satanic force lies in the fact that "temptation either seems to come, or actually comes, with a personal seduction,"[9] in other words, by a force outside ourselves. This, however, makes it all too easy to excuse our own evil acts by laying the blame elsewhere. Indeed, our court system is deluged by persons maintaining that they were under the influence of "diminished capacity" or "mental illness" at the time they committed the crimes for which they were arrested. It is one of the reasons that this defense is being reexamined and weakened in some quarters today.

Probably the most deeply rooted dualistic approach to suffering has been in that view of the atonement, which defines the death of Christ as a ransom paid to

Satan for the sins of humankind.[10] But the same question can be raised of this theory that was raised earlier with regard to the concept of omnipotence. What kind of God has to submit a Son to Satan simply to satisfy that God's own wrath? And could not an omnipotent God devise a less costly, less painful means of fulfilling the divine will?

One's preference for a particular approach to the problem of suffering may come down to a matter of individual theological persuasion. But for me, to say to a bereaved family, "Your son's death was due to Satan's power, but God will make it right in the end," leaves too many questions unanswered. That approach is devoid of present hope and consolation.

SUFFERING: A HELP IN PERCEIVING GOODNESS

Another well-known approach to suffering can be found in Alan Paton's brief essay, "Why Suffering?" He wrote that

> all who are mature, whether young or old, accept suffering as inseparable from life; even if it is not experienced, the possibility of it is always there. I myself cannot even conceive of life without suffering. I cannot even conceive that life could have meaning without suffering. There would certainly be no music, no theatre, no literature, no art. I suspect that the alternative to a universe in which there is suffering, in which evil struggles with good and cruelty with mercy, would be a universe of nothingness . . . only an eternity of uninterrupted banality.[11]

In other words, suffering is instrumental in our appreciation of life. Moreover, it could be said that we never fully appreciate goodness without evil or good health without suffering.

We must admit that there is a measure of truth in this approach. How much more do we appreciate the beauty of a sunny day when it comes after several days of socked-in-gray and rainy weather! It can even be admitted that pain plays a necessary part in helping us to stay healthy. It was the painful experience of being burned by a hot radiator that taught our oldest son to stay away from the hot pipes. It was my own pain that alerted my parents to a serious condition that resulted in the removal of my appendix.

Indeed, some of us choose to face danger in order to accent our experience of life. An acquaintance of mine loves to ride his motorcycle at high speed. My inclination is to say to him that anyone who rides one of those things has to be crazy. His response recognizes the danger involved, but sees in that very danger an element of excitement that lends zest to his life. On one occasion, when I gave voice to my feelings, he said, "Yes, I know it's dangerous, but knowing that I have total control over my life as I hold on to the handlebars gives me a thrill that I've never known in any other way." Similar feelings might well be voiced by athletes who, despite the recognized possibility of injury, persist in their sport to the point of achieving a level of performance never before reached by anyone else. Ralph Sockman once wrote: "A world without hardships would be unendurable."[12]

Though our experience may confirm the truth of what we have said, we must still test this as an approach of explaining suffering. How much truth does it possess? A great many people, for example, who love to ride motorcycles are injured or killed by a momentary loss of control. Professional athletes, striving for peak performance, sustain crippling injuries, some of which affect them for the remainder of their lives. If we look at such monstrous examples of suffering as that of the Jews of Europe during World War II, it is virtually impossible for us to identify any possible good that came out of the anguish that took place. Author Annie Dillard, commenting on Jesus' healing of the blind man and his attendant explanation that the man was born blind in order that the "works of God should be made manifest," asked "Do we really need more victims to remind us that we're all victims?"[13]

A few years ago, I visited Israel's memorial to the Holocaust, Yad Vashem. I entered by the quiet lane lined with trees planted in memory of those who, at risk to their own lives, sheltered Jews from the Nazis. I remembered an often-heard suggestion that the memorial stands as a constant reminder of the terrible inhumanity of which groups of people are capable of perpetrating on other persons. But my feeling was not that I was glad the memorial was there. Rather, I felt terribly saddened by the events that made such a memorial necessary. Even as I compared the two *bas-relief* portrayals of the Warsaw ghetto tragedy—one depicting the anguish of those being herded onto cattle cars, the other capturing the defiance in the faces of those who led the Ghetto revolt—my sense of sadness was not lessened by the courage evident in the portrayal of those who resisted.

Sheldon Vanauken, in his chronicle of his relationship with his wife Davy and of her untimely death, remarked that

> goodness and love are as real as their terrible opposites, and, in truth, far more real, though I say this mindful of the enormous evils like Nazi Germany. But love is the final reality; and anyone who does not understand this, be he writer or sage, is a man flawed in wisdom.[14]

But there are those who permanently lose their faith in all goodness as a result of such intense evil. The question is real: What possible good can be occasioned by such enormous evil? Though truth is to be found in the enhancement of good through pain, as an explanation for the problem of suffering, it still leaves something to be desired.

SUFFERING: A PUNISHMENT FOR SIN

The notion that suffering is the means God chooses to punish persons for sin remains influential in the minds of many in the church. An outgrowth of the Old Testament Deuteronomic Code's requirement of an eye-for-an-eye, the doctrine can be found in many places. It is particularly evident in the prophetic literature. The prophet Amos, called by God to preach God's judgment upon Israel for that nation's failure to live up to its covenant with God, began his attack by reminding the Israelites of God's special relationship with them.

> You only have I known
>   of all the families of the earth;
> therefore I will punish you
>   for all you iniquities.
>
> (Amos 3:2)

The concept persisted into New Testament times, even as Jesus went about revising the Deuteronomic

Code. In John's story of the healing of the man born blind, the disciples asked Jesus: "Rabbi, who sinned, this man or his parents, that he was born blind?" (John 9:2). The notion can still be found in our churches today. I vividly remember the bereaved parents of an infant who was born with a severe birth defect. Because the child had been conceived out of wedlock, the parents were convinced that God had taken their baby's life to punish them for their sin. Joseph Heller's recent novel, *God Knows,* speaks in a similar vein. Expressing King David's anger at God for taking the life of the child born of the adulterous affair with Bathsheba, Heller wrote:

> There is never, *never* any mercy to be expected from heaven. I have still not forgiven God for getting back at me that way, and I know I never shall, no matter how much He begs me, not if He begs me for a million years. . . . He lifts the blame from me and kills the guiltless child. Now *there's* an original sin for you.[15]

The idea that God sends suffering as a punishment for sin relies primarily on a view of God shared by most of the theories we have examined thus far. Far from the New Testament's loving God, revealed among us in Jesus Christ, such a punishing God remains transcendent, possesses all knowledge and power, and does not hesitate in using power to achieve certain ends, however mysterious those ends may seem to us. As Wallace Fisher contends, "God, without violating human freedom, can and does allow, and occasionally sends, suffering in order to discipline a person, to correct his human defects, to bring a 'good' life into a position where it can accept him."[16] There are others,

47

however, who find this interpretation of suffering to be extremely repugnant. Dorothee Soelle, for example, believes that such a God is little more than a theological sadist.[17]

The concept has a number of problems. It is impossible to account for all instances of suffering as evidences of sin. It is preposterous to suggest, for example, that people living in impoverished nations die of starvation because God sends famine to punish them for their sin. Natural disasters do not easily yield to this kind of explanation. And what about children who suffer and die before ever learning what sin is all about? In *J.B.*, Job's wife protests to her husband:

> God is just!
> If God is just our slaughtered children
> Stank with sin, were rotten with it! . . .
>   They are
> Dead and they were innocent: I will not
> Let you sacrifice their deaths
> To make injustice justice and God good![18]

There often seems to be no correlation between the quality of a person's life and the degree of suffering experienced by that person. We have seen evil people receive punishments that seemed better than they deserved, and we have seen suffering visited upon good people who, on this theory, should have been protected. Consider further the death of Jesus. Are we to conclude that the agony of crucifixion was the result of an unfaithful life? What of our own lives? Could we, as Buttrick said,

endure a God of strict justice? Do we not hope for more than justice? Imagine him keeping a million celestial ledgers, his world filled with millions of invisible detective accounts!

Could we love God on those terms? Would there be any
courage or faith in such a world, or even kindness? Would not
goodness vanish in a prudential resolve to keep on the right
side of the ledger?[19]

Indeed it might. Furthermore, when suffering is seen
as a punishment for sin, it often produces guilt in the
most undeserving persons, if it has not already led to an
outright rejection of God. The entire book of Job and the
life of Christ stand as a repudiation of the concept that
suffering is to be explained in terms of sin. It is time for
such a generalization to die a well-deserved death.

SUFFERING: FROM THE MISUSE
OF HUMAN FREEDOM

Another approach that requires analysis is similar to
the dualistic philosophy, which accounts for suffering
through the work of a satanic figure. The focus of this
approach is on freedom of the will. Its roots can be
traced back to Augustine (A.D. 354–430).

The argument traces most suffering to persons'
misuse of their God-given gift of freedom. In answer to
those who would question God's wisdom in granting
so much freedom, it is argued that such freedom is
necessary for persons to make meaningful choices in
order to follow God's leading. In a deterministic
philosophy, there is no need for ethical guidance, since
all actions would be predetermined and inevitable.
Instead, we have been created with freedom, whereby
we can accept or reject God's leading. Only so is it
possible for us to respond to God out of love. The risk
arises at the point at which we are free to reject God and

49

to choose to do evil. One of this theory's proponents, Stephen T. Davis, suggests that "unfortunately, this is just what [people] did: they chose to go wrong; they fell into sin. So God is not to be blamed for the existence of evil in the world—we are." At first blush, our response is to ask, "Who? Me?" Are we to assume *all* of the blame? Must not God bear a share of the blame as well? Apparently not, for as Davis writes, God is only

> *indirectly* responsible for evil in the sense that he created the conditions given which evil would come into existence . . . and he foreknew the evil choices we would make. . . .
>
> [But] God's decision will turn out to be wise because the good that will in the end result from his decision will outweigh the evil that will in the end result from it. In the eschaton it will be seen that God chose the best course and that the favorable balance of good over evil that will then exist was obtainable by God in no other way.[20]

What of evil that does not result from human causality, such as natural disasters? Alvin Plantinga suggests that "the natural evil we find is due to the free actions of nonhuman spirits."[21]

While we may be uncertain as to the extent to which suffering is caused by "nonhuman spirits," there is little doubt that much pain can be attributed to human agency. The acts of terrorism that stain our world bring untold suffering to families touched by their barbarity. Who can look at Picasso's "Guernica" without feeling a sense of sadness at the violence brought upon nations in times of war? The destruction of Hiroshima and Nagasaki, the obliteration of a previously unheard of hamlet that put Mi Lai into common parlance, the American persecution of black people and Native

Americans, and the overwhelming horror of Auschwitz all testify to human freedom gone amok. All such pain and suffering lend credence to Paul's belief that "all have sinned and fall short of the glory of God" (Rom. 3:23). When we recognize the evil of which we are capable, there is no doubt that the "costliest aspect of creation is letting the creatures be."[22]

That, however, is also the most telling argument against the plausibility of explaining suffering primarily in terms of the misuse of human freedom. S. Paul Schilling asked the key question:

> Is moral freedom really so worthful that it outweighs other values like life, happiness, aesthetic appreciation, and justice, which are sacrificed when free will is allowed to run its course? . . . Why must there be so much liberty that some individuals can become thoroughly depraved?[23]

It can be argued that the amount of freedom given to us by our Creator is more than we are able to handle in a responsible and righteous manner. To suggest, however, as Alvin Plantinga does, that the more aberrant examples of suffering are due, not so much to human causality, as to the work of "non-human forces" still leaves us with a pre-scientific and unsatisfactory world view. Some, in response, will claim that instances of suffering on the scale of the Holocaust require more of an explanation than free will is capable of providing and will look toward an eschatological solution. Others, such as Frederick Sontag, will simply say that "We have seen so much waste to date that neither a utopia on earth nor a heavenly existence later could justify it."[24] In short, this explanation leaves more than its share of questions unanswered.

It is essential for us to examine each approach in terms of its ability to speak to the pain and questions that are brought into the lives of those who suffer. Suffering that defies any attempt to explain it in terms of the misuse of human freedom cannot be approached in that manner.

SUFFERING: A MEANS OF TESTING

The last concept we will examine here is in many ways the most appealing. It seems to contain a large measure of truth and to be grounded in scripture. As the writer of the Epistle to the Hebrews expressed it: "It is for discipline that you have to endure. God is treating you as sons; for what son is there whom his father does not discipline?" (Heb. 12:7).

Suffering, from this perspective, can be interpreted as the means by which God tests, challenges, or attempts to teach us. So seen, it becomes a means whereby we may learn a lesson. Suffering can be the way in which God brings us to obedience, enabling us to learn to live in accordance with the divine will.

One of the best-known apostles of this position has been C. S. Lewis. In *The Great Divorce*, he comments on a mother's questions of God following the death of her son, Michael. Says Lewis, God wanted

> your merely instinctive love for your child . . . to turn into something better. He wanted you to love Michael as He understands love. You cannot love a fellow creature fully till you love God. Sometimes this conversion can be done while the instinctive love is still gratified. But there was, it seems, no chance of that in your case. . . . The only remedy was to take away the object. It was a case for surgery.[25]

More recently, we find the same theme contained in letters that passed between author Sheldon Vanauken and Lewis, published in Vanauken's *A Severe Mercy*. Following the death of Vanauken's wife, Lewis wrote (almost harshly) that

> One Flesh must not (and in the long run cannot) "live to itself" any more than the single individual. It was made for God and (in Him) for its neighbors—first and foremost among them the children it ought to have produced. . . . One way or another the thing had to die. Perpetual springtime is not allowed. . . . You have been treated with a severe mercy. You have been brought to see . . . that you were jealous of God.[26]

In attempting to create the perfect relationship with his wife, Davy, and through her subsequent death, Vanauken—with Lewis' help—became convinced that God had taken Davy as a means of teaching him that love for God must take precedence over love shared with another person.

This seems, indeed, to be a "severe mercy," if mercy it be. However, some good things can be said about this understanding of suffering. Pain, for example, can be the way in which our aging bodies remind us that they are not well-served by a sedentary existence. We can think of people in whom pain has awakened a need for medical care, giving them a longer and fuller life. We have known some whose lives were being ruined by a chemical dependency and who believed that the experience of "hitting bottom" was the means God chose to reveal to them their need for help. There have been athletes who, out of their belief that God was testing their endurance, went from painful setbacks to new heights of achievement. History is replete with examples of physicians who, after contracting or treating a severe illness, were driven to discover a cure for that illness. Quite ordinary people are moved in a moment of extreme danger to levels of endurance and courage that they would never have suspected they possessed. Many of us have found our lives uplifted by the witness of persons who, despite severe pain, managed to develop a much greater degree of hope, trust, and faith in God's goodness. Often, those who would seem to have the most reason to question the goodness of the Creator have become, instead, the strongest proponents of God's love. Ralph Sockman spoke for most of us when he said that "we are immeasurably helped by those who do not crack up when they might be expected to do so."[27]

Even the briefest of glances into the pages of scripture makes it quite evident that there is a basis for this view of suffering. Abraham's agony in his willingness to sacrifice Isaac, the wilderness wanderings of Moses and the Israelites, Jesus' temptation experience, and Paul's discovery that God's strength is "made perfect in weakness" (II Cor. 2:9) have helped many of us to survive the "dark night of the soul" and to go on to a renewed vision of our calling.

Having said all that, we must raise other questions of this view of suffering. While we can appreciate Abraham's dedication and total trust in the God who asked him to sacrifice his son, we also find ourselves inclined to wonder what kind of God puts a parent through such pain, even if issuing a reprieve at the last minute? Where some would find Abraham's witness admirable, others, like Dorothee Soelle, find in that story a God "insensitive to human misery," a God who "holds contempt for humanity."[28]

While great medical advances have undoubtedly been made through the suffering and death of generations of people, what of the millions of persons who suffered and died before a cure was discovered? What of infants who, like our son, died without a diagnosis ever made as to what sort of malady took his life?

There is also a problem at the point of natural evil. When an earthquake claims the lives of thousands of people, can anyone honestly believe that God was challenging or testing the faith of all of those who died? For those who find in such natural disasters a challenge by God for us to "conquer and subdue" the world, there are others who, like John A. T. Robinson, when looking at such disasters, believe that

> the idea that there is any intention or plan about their incidence is . . . sheer blasphemy. Nowhere in that great meditation of suffering and evil in Romans 8 does St. Paul ever suggest that these things disclose the purpose of God . . . their chief quality is what St. Paul calls "vanity"— meaningless, purposeless futility.[29]

Even C. S. Lewis, who may later have had cause to rethink his position following the loss of his own wife, wrote approvingly to Sheldon Vanauken of the "vision of our Lord that said to St. Theresa on some frightful occasion, 'This is how I always treat my friends.' Her response to God is instructive. 'Then Lord, it is not surprising that You have so few.' "[30]

It is obvious that some instances of suffering may well be endured or explained by viewing them as a means of testing by God. It is also plain that this approach to the problem does not speak meaningfully to all instances of suffering.

Perhaps, expecting an approach to the problem of suffering to cover all these bases is not realistic. However, some other attempts at understanding suffering have gathered more followers and have enjoyed a wider acceptance over the course of time. For many of us who must deal with the problem, such explanations offer more help than the approaches we have examined thus far. We turn next to them.

Notes

1. One of the most thorough of recent volumes is S. Paul Schilling's *God and Human Anguish* (Nashville: Abingdon Press, 1977).

2. Archibald MacLeish, *J.B.* (Cambridge, Mass.: Houghton Mifflin, 1986), p. 121.

3. Schilling, *God and Human Anguish*, pp. 69-71.

4. Paul Scherer, exposition of the book of Job, in *The Interpreter's Bible*, ed. Nolan B. Harmon, vol. III (New York: Abingdon Press, 1954), p. 914.

5. Arthur C. McGill, *Suffering*, with foreword by Paul Ramsey and William F. May (Philadelphia: Westminster Press, 1982), pp. 20-21.

6. Ibid., p. 36.

7. Ibid., pp. 47, 86.

8. Ibid., p. 92.

9. George A. Buttrick, *God, Pain, and Evil* (Nashville: Abingdon Press, 1966), p. 64.

10. For a more complete discussion of this view, see Schilling, *God and Human Anguish*, p. 110.

11. Alan Paton, "Why Suffering?" In *Creative Suffering: The Ripple of Hope* (Kansas City: National Catholic Reporter Publishing Co., 1970), p. 15.

12. Ralph Sockman, *The Meaning of Suffering* (New York: Abingdon Press, 1961), p. 66.

13. Annie Dillard, *Holy the Firm* (New York: Harper, 1984), p. 60.

14. Sheldon Vanauken, *A Severe Mercy* (London: Hodder and Stoughton, 1970), p. 164.

15. Joseph Heller, *God Knows* (New York: Alfred A. Knopf, 1984), p. 81.

16. Wallace Fisher, "Why Must People Suffer?" In *Preaching the Passion*, ed. Alton M. Motter (Philadelphia: Fortress Press, 1963), p. 21.

17. Dorothee Soelle, *Suffering*, trans. Everett R. Kalin (Philadelphia: Fortress Press, 1975), pp. 22-29.

18. MacLeish, *J.B.*, pp. 109-10.

19. Buttrick, *God, Pain, and Evil*, p. 34.

20. Stephen T. Davis, "Free Will and Evil." In *Encountering Evil* (Atlanta: John Knox Press, 1981), pp. 70-71.

21. Alvin Plantinga, *God, Freedom, and Evil* (New York: Harper, 1974), p. 58.

22. Geddes MacGregor, *He Who Lets Us Be* (New York: Seabury Press, 1975), p. 136.

23. Schilling, *God and Human Anguish*, p. 203.

24. Frederick Sontag, Critique of Davis' "Free Will and Evil." In *Encountering Evil*, ed. Stephen T. Davis (Atlanta: John Knox Press, 1981), p. 85.

25. C. S. Lewis, *The Great Divorce* (New York: Macmillan, 1941), p. 92.

26. Vanauken, *A Severe Mercy*, p. 210.

27. Sockman, *The Meaning of Suffering*, p. 89.

28. Soelle, *Suffering*, p. 26.

29. John A. T. Robinson, "Evil and the God of Love." In *To God Be the Glory*, ed. Theodore A. Gill (Nashville: Abingdon Press, 1973), p. 27.

30. Vanauken, *A Severe Mercy*, p. 186.

Chapter Three
A Two-story Universe

"I feel need of shriv'ness, Father—and something else as well."
"Something else, Mrs. Grales?"
She leaned closer to whisper behind her hand, "I need be giving
shriv'ness to Him, as well."
The priest recoiled slightly. "To whom? I don't understand."
"Shriv'ness—to Him who made me as I am."

A Canticle for Leibowitz by Walter M. Miller, Jr.

True, since we are thrown into history at our birth, we appear in
social settings made by human hands, but ultimately those hands
cannot account for themselves. To the extent that they are born with
the potential and the power to be dirty, credit for that fact belongs
elsewhere. "Elsewhere" is God's address.

"A Theodicy of Protest," John K. Roth

Now and then a terminal disease ennobles; most of the time it is miles
from being even the best of a bad job. To set God up as an instrument
who uses such methods, is to make him the warden of the worst-run
penitentiary of all. The atheist who would rather have no God makes far
more sense than the pietist who will take that kind of injustice lying
down. The atheist at least sounds like Job; the pietist sounds like hell.

The Third Peacock, Robert Farrar Capon

In all these things we are more than conquerors through him who
loved us. (Romans 8:37)

59

Her name was Jean. She was an attractive, vivacious thirty-two-year-old high school teacher and cheerleading coach. I might never have met her if it had not been for the fact that one of our church members just happened to be placed in the same hospital room with Jean. Through the concern of our parishioner, I learned that Jean was there to have a mastectomy to remove a tumor from her breast. As no pastor had called on her, I introduced myself, expressed my concern, and our relationship began. It was to continue over the course of almost two years, during which time she experienced more surgery, all of the painful side effects of chemotherapy, more suffering through other illnesses in addition to her cancer, and, eventually, death.

A bright and articulate young woman, she was able to talk freely about her cancer, and even on occasion make light of her condition. But there were many other tearful conversations, particularly those that touched on her impending death and its impact on her husband and two young children. The injustice of it all never left us, even though, at the end, she died peacefully. Her cancer had, by that time, reduced her to a state that scarcely reflected life. When death came, it was a blessing. But those of us who knew and came to love Jean found ourselves deeply angry—angry at God, angry at society's inability to discover a cure for this dreaded killer, angry at our fragile mortality.

A DIFFERENT UNDERSTANDING
OF OMNIPOTENCE

The experience of anger is familiar to many pastors, having shared it with suffering and bereaved families in the parish. The time comes, however, when one must look beyond the bitter feelings to the need for bringing a word of hope. Such a word can be brought out of an understanding of suffering that springs from a different definition of omnipotence from those we have seen in theories examined so far and that unites elements from several similar positions.

Traditionally, we have understood God's omnipotence to mean that God can do anything, anytime, in any place, without regard for what appear to us to be natural laws. If need be, God can part the waters of the Red Sea and enable the Hebrews to pass dry-shod from the land of their captivity. God can cause the walls of Jericho to crumble, send fire to consume Elijah's sacrifice, and enlist the heathen Cyrus to discipline his chosen people. This transcendent, austere, and vengeful Creator is no deity to take lightly, as countless Old Testament figures learned to their own chagrin!

Though we may anchor this concept of God in the Old Testament, it is also an understanding that is very much a part of the minds of many who make up our congregations. It is the source of a great many problems at the point of trying to deal with the mystery of pain. When contemporary authors, such as Annie Dillard, describe the high degree of violence and suffering in nature, we may wonder whether God has a plan for creation and, if so, how all of nature's violence could possibly be a part of it. The randomness of the violence would seem to argue against any sort of divine intention. It suggests chaos rather than order.

The inequitable distribution of suffering causes us to raise questions of God's goodness as well as about the efficacy of faith. If God is somehow in control of all that is, yet freely allows suffering to afflict the most righteous of his servants, then of what use is belief in such a God? It might be argued that the purposes of an all-powerful God are, by necessity, too great for us to understand but that God will make all things right in the end. But the intensity of some suffering seems to defy any purpose, however great it might be. It is difficult to understand how any purpose could transform the horror of the Holocaust. Those who feel that suffering is instrumental in the creation of discipline and courage must deal with the objection offered by others who, looking at the suffering, would prefer not to be disciplined or brave. The cost simply seems to be too great. In short, Paul Tillich may have been correct in his assessment that

> only the almighty God can be man's ultimate concern. A very mighty God may claim to be of ultimate concern; but he is not, and his claim comes to naught, because he cannot resist nonbeing and therefore he cannot supply the ultimate courage which conquers anxiety.[1]

On the other hand, if as pastors we are to deal meaningfully and faithfully with suffering, "we must reexamine what can be meant by an infinite degree of power," because as soon as we "ascribe such unlimited power to God, we make him seem like a monster."[2] Clearly, we need to understand the quality of omnipotence in a new or different sense.

THE PROCESS APPROACH

Insight for this approach can be found in a number of quarters, but chiefly in the school of thought that has come to be known as "process theology." Let us begin to examine this at the point of the creation itself, regarding the creation not as a finished product, but as a product engaged in a continual process of becoming. In the Revised Standard Version of the Bible, a note to the opening verse of the book of Genesis informs us that an alternative reading suggests that in the beginning God *began* to create the heavens and the earth. David R. Griffin has argued that an acceptance of this alternative reading enables us to view God's creation of our world not as "the absolute beginning of finite existence but rather the achievement of order out of a pre-existing chaos."[3] While God's power, evidenced in the Creation, is "essentially unlimited," it is not absolute, as God worked with "some pre-existent actualities . . . [with] power of their own with which they could partially thwart the divine will."[4] Further, God created each of us as free beings, endowed with the ability to determine what sort of persons we will become. In order for us to develop fully our potential as persons, it was necessary to place us within a stable environment, but yet an environment that inherently contained conditions that constantly challenged us to take part in God's creative activity of making the world a more human and humane place. The means by which God chose to achieve this end was that of loving persuasion. God sought to "lure the creatures to realize the greatest good that is possible" in every given situation.[5]

It is immediately obvious that persons may choose to ignore God's leading, giving rise to all sorts of suffering as a result of their misguided activity. The blame for this, however, cannot be laid at God's door, since the creation of persons who were not free to make their own choices would have consigned them to a life of slavish obedience and meaningless servitude. As it is, persons are free to experience all of the challenge of becoming loving, creative, and just individuals who freely follow God's lead.

The God whose will we seek to learn and whose love moves us to follow him is no austere, vengeful, and extremely transcendent unmoved Mover. He is, rather, a God who is vulnerable. Daniel Day Williams has written of a God who knows that "to love is to be vulnerable—vulnerable to the hurts and risks that come from setting the other free and accepting his freedom."[6] For while that freedom can be the source of violence, it can also be the originator of healing.

Inasmuch as change is a slow process, requiring much experimentation, there is an element of suffering that is an inevitable part of that process. The development of a cure for devastating illness will lead researchers to follow leads that do not pan out and that leave suffering in their wake. Technology, which seeks to create a better world, will make mistakes, unintentionally causing suffering as a result of those errors. The development of nuclear power has freed us in some measure from raping the land in search of fossil fuels, but not without the threat of a Chernobyl. It may seem that a great deal has been left to chance in such an arrangement, but who can look at the scientific achievements of the last thirty years without arguing that living conditions have become better? As for suffering that is caused by natural forces,

> if God has always worked with materials that were not necessarily in a perfect state, and which have some inherent power to deviate from God's aims . . . there is no reason to infer that cancer, polio, tornadoes, and earthquakes exist because God wanted our world to have them.[7]

Unlike those who might view such disasters as the work of Satan or nonhuman spirits, we see them here as simply an inevitable part of a universe that is in a state of flux, that yearns to "be set free from its bondage to decay" and is "groaning in travail" (Rom. 8:21-22).

Such an approach to the problem of suffering is not without its questions. Limiting the power of God in such a way has been compared to having "God on a leash."[8] On the other hand, such limiting seems quite compatible with the God whose "power is made perfect in weakness" (II Cor. 12:9). The God whose life was lived by Jesus to its cruciform conclusion and whose life is characterized by the loving of one's enemies and doing good to those who persecute us seems to be a God of vulnerability. If vulnerability makes some feel that God is weak, there are others, such as Gabriel Fackre, who find meaningful a

> divine vulnerability that risks the abuse of freedom by a covenant partner but patiently and stubbornly pursues a rebel creation. The power of God is reconceived in the light of the central chapter of the story in which "the weakness of God proves stronger than men . . . in cross and resurrection.[9]

John Hick, whose major approach to theodicy has yet to be examined, has argued that a process approach, which limits the power of God, amounts to nothing more than a denial of the existence of the problem of evil.[10] That is, the qualifying of God's power relieves us of the task of trying to reconcile the presence of suffering with a God who has the power to relieve it, but apparently does not seem willing to exercise that power.

There is some truth to Hick's objection. His contention, however, rests on one definition of that power. As S. Paul Schilling has noted:

> To regard divine power as less than infinite does not mean to think of God as weak and puny. His power is not absolute, but it is utterly unparalleled. He is the source, ground, and possessor of all the power . . . he needs for the ultimate attainment of his righteous purposes. Moreover, the unbounded love that animates all his work is its own unique strength. He gains his ends less by coercion than by self-sacrificial effort to lead his creatures toward freely chosen fulfillment of his will.[11]

What is at issue here is not so much a matter of degree of power as it is a matter of purpose, God's purpose. As Leslie Weatherhead clearly saw, "God's power is not put forward to get certain things done, but to get them done in a certain way, and with certain results in the lives of those who do them."[12]

At this point, then, it seems worthwhile to look at Hick's approach. Although he would not adopt the process approach to the problem, he has had much to say about God's *purpose* in allowing his creation to be exposed to suffering.

With Hick, the word *process* occurs again, but within the context of human growth. Where, as we have seen, Griffin believes the world to have been created in an unfinished state, Hick believes that human beings were not created in "a finished state" and are "still in the process of creation."[13] He posits a two-stage concept of the creation of humankind, first "in the 'image' and then in the 'likeness' of God." At the creation, people were created in a state of moral and spiritual immaturity, a kind of unfinished clay. Ahead of them lay a long process of growth in which all engaged in the task of becoming "intelligent, ethical, and religious" creatures through free choices made in response to God's overtures.[14]

Those who look at the suffering involved in our struggle to follow God's lead might ask why God did not simply create all of us moral to begin with. Hick's answer, similar to other approaches we have examined, is that the struggle to follow God's lead requires a state of freedom for those choices to have any value. Further, our individual characters are tried, tested, and toughened by the suffering we undergo in the process of becoming.

As for natural evil, Hick's position is similar to Griffin's. The world in which we have been placed, with all of its hazards, still represents the best environment to stimulate our growth toward maturity.

A serious criticism of Hick's position is that of cost effectiveness. The sheer intensity of the evil present in our world seems to far exceed any possible benefit we might derive from our struggle with it. At this point, however, Hick introduces an eschatological element, his belief that "this person-making process leading eventually to perfect human community, is not completed on this earth."[15] Here again we are subject to the questions of those who find an eschatological belief hard to understand, given a starting assumption of God's infinite power. If God's power is absolute, why could he not just complete his purpose of leading us to maturity in this life? Why let us finish our lives with the frustration of unanswered questions and the question of whether the struggle has been worthwhile?

When, however, one accepts a limitation on the power possessed by God, then this question does not arise with the same force. If we begin with a two-story universe, containing elements antithetical to God with a power of their own, in which we are part of a creation, moving from one story to another in search of maturity, the eschatological element offers us the hope of ultimate triumph over the mystery of present pain. A view somewhat similar to this was taken by the writer to the Hebrews, with regard to his predecessors in the faith. He noted that all of these people, "Though well attested by their faith, did not receive what was promised, since God had foreseen something better for us, that apart from us they should not be made perfect" (Heb. 11:39-40).

An additional question remains, however: Where is God in the process of our becoming? While we are struggling with the suffering that is an inevitable part of an imperfect world, is God sitting impassibly by, saddened that his creatures must undergo such pain, but unwilling or unable to do anything about it? If that is the case, then we might well be justified in refusing to follow God and in learning to live as insulated and secure a life as we possibly can. That is not the case, however, and here we must introduce the part played by God's involvement through Jesus Christ, for, as Alan Paton put it, "These are questions that cannot be answered in an article or a book, but only in a life."[16]

One of the most poignant and courageous sermons

that I have read recently was that delivered by William Sloane Coffin shortly after the death of his son, Alex. Speaking to those who find the will of God in such events, Coffin wrote:

> Nothing so infuriates me as the incapacity of seemingly intelligent people to get it through their heads that God doesn't go around in this world with his finger on triggers, his fist around knives, his hands on steering wheels. God is dead set against all unnatural deaths. And Christ spent an inordinate amount of time delivering people from paralysis, insanity, leprosy, and muteness. . . . The one thing that should never be said when someone dies is, "It is the will of God." Never do we know enough to say that. My own consolation lies in knowing that it was not the will of God that Alex die; that when the waves closed over the sinking car, God's heart was the first of all our hearts to break.[17]

Where is God when we go through the agony of unexplained suffering? The answer for many theologians is that God is present in that suffering with us, sharing it with us and hurting as deeply as we do.

The notion that God can suffer with us falls somewhat strangely upon modern ears. It seems to be an echo of the old Patripassionist heresy, which was vigorously rejected by the early church. Recent work, however, such as Jürgen Moltmann's *The Crucified God*, has brought back the understanding that "those who follow [Christ] suffer and die in fellowship with him."[18]

In the Old Testament, God is portrayed as being actively involved in the life of his people. It is God who was with Moses and the Israelites, sustaining them in their post-Sinai journey through the wilderness. It is God who was with Elijah, not only in Mt. Carmel's triumph, but also in the loneliness of Beersheba. Not

69

only was God actively involved in the life of his people when they were obedient and following him, but he also journeyed with them into exile. In the New Testament, we witness God actively at work in the ministry of Jesus and fully present in the agony of the crucifixion.

Admittedly, the concept of a God who suffers may seem strange to those who, as Dorothee Soelle notes, inherit "the ancient belief in an a-patheic God, one unmoved by anything."[19] But if, as I have suggested, God has chosen a more costly means of achieving purposes, to be subjected with the creation to suffering while preserving our freedom to choose for him, then "the costliness of God's efforts" implies also "that he shares deeply the anguish of his creation" and "When his creatures suffer for whatever reason, he not only knows about their suffering but concretely experiences it."[20]

How, then, can this approach to suffering aid us as pastors in dealing with the problem as we encounter it in the lives of our parishioners? I believe that it offers us many more possibilities than the approaches previously examined, possibilities that are validated every day in our ministry with the suffering and dying.

First, the approach enjoys the benefit of a solid scriptural base. Jesus described his Father's work as incomplete and ongoing (John 5:17). Paul described a universe that was in a process of change and needed to be set free from its bondage and travail (Rom. 8:21 ff.). Under such a situation of continuing creation, the rain falls on the righteous and the unrighteous alike (Matt. 5:45).

Second, the suffering that is a part of creation's groaning contributes toward our development as mature sons and daughters of God. The story of the testing of Abraham in Genesis 22 conveys a picture of a man whose loyalty and trust in God have developed to the point where he is willing to risk all that he loves. The letter of James makes a point of stressing that the undergoing of trials serves to produce firmness in belief and determination (1:2-5). Paul, who suffered again and again for his faith and missional activity, was able to suggest that we should rejoice when we suffer because of the endurance, character, and hope that can come from such experiences (Rom. 5:3-4).

Third, this approach focuses on a God who is near to us. The church has always believed that God was in Christ and fully understood life as we live it.[21] The Isaiah Servant Songs have been interpreted to be indicative of Christ's suffering. According to Isaiah, the Servant has known the frustration of laboring in vain in the face of a people who would not listen to him (49:4); he has been persecuted in the most shameful way, while not turning his back on those he would save (50:6); he has been "despised and rejected by men," "acquainted with grief," "wounded for our transgressions," and "numbered with the transgressors" (53:3-12). In the Garden of Gethsemane, Jesus' "agony" in prayer became "like great drops of blood falling down upon the ground" (Luke 22:44). Before the tomb of Lazarus, "Jesus wept" in great sadness (John 11:35). Beaten by the Roman guards to within a shadow of dying, he was led through the streets of Jerusalem outside the city wall to the cross and the crucifixion's ultimate experience of alienation and pain. Surely, we are brought to agree with Isaiah's judgment that "he has borne our griefs and carried our sorrows" (53:4). Surely we must share with Martin Marty the judgment that "God *participates* in the life of the people and suffers at their side, thus meriting [our] trust."[22]

It could be argued that this portrait of God offers us little hope, that there is no reason for us to "welcome enthusiastically" a God who seems to have "no plan, no power and no precedent to kindle" our anticipation of better times.[23] But to speak in that fashion is to render meaningless the Resurrection, experienced by Jesus and promised to us through faith in Christ. Indeed, there is the greatest of reasons for us to believe that God loves us and can be trusted to make all things right. As William Stringfellow put it:

> To become and be a beneficiary of the Resurrection of Jesus Christ means . . . freedom *now* from all conformities to death, freedom *now* from fear of the power of death, freedom *now* from the bondage of idolatry to death, freedom *now* to live in hope while awaiting the Judgment.[24]

The knowledge that God is not unaffected by our suffering, that he shares it with us, does indeed set us free to approach it in a new and more helpful fashion. Pastors have seen such freeing take place in the lives of those who suffer.

Fourth, this approach makes a difference *now*. The awareness of God's presence often serves to lend strength and courage to persons facing pain. I have called on such persons in the hospital, intending to try to lift their spirits. I have left their hospital rooms, feeling that they have ministered to me in a deep way, helping me to deal with my own feelings of mortality and uncertainty, impressing me with the depth of their faith. Such was the case with Jean, whose story began this chapter. She not only evidenced a courage of which I knew nothing, but she also felt that God was helping her to accept her impending death with the belief that somehow all would be well.

Strength may also be found in the knowledge that we are not alone in the moment of our dying. I remember vividly the death of a man who had served in the armed forces in the Pacific during World War II. His acquaintance with suffering and death came from holding the hands of his comrades as they suffered and died from their wounds. He firmly believed that there was no lonelier moment in life than the moment when we know we are dying. He had virtually dedicated himself to being with others when their wounds brought them to that point. Yet, when that moment came for him, he shared with me his feeling that he was not alone. Somehow, though he could not find the words to explain it, he felt himself very much in the presence of God and was able to approach his dying without fear.

"God is here," said a woman who had undergone a bone marrow transplant in the hope of stemming her leukemia. "He knows what my pain is like," she said, and from that derived a measure of strength that enabled her to keep up her spirit and inspire those who treated her.

"I'll make it," said a young father whose cancer was slowly taking his life. He knew that nothing could be done for him, but he wanted to hold up long enough to say goodbye to his children, who hadn't seen him since he entered the hospital for treatment. He did make it and shared with me and with his physician his belief that God had been with him, sharing the load of his pain, giving him the "space" he needed.

Time and again, I have had that experience with suffering persons. I have shared with them my belief that God hurts with us, that a part of the meaning of Jesus' title, Emmanuel (God with us), has to do with God's presence and sharing in the midst of our pain. To his disciples, Jesus said, "Lo, I am with you always, even to the close of the age" (Matt. 28:20). I have no doubt that in the years of intense persecution that followed there were many occasions on which they remembered those words and took comfort from them.

Fifth, the knowledge that suffering is a natural part of our world that is shared by God also frees us to identify with those who suffer and enables us to take part in their struggle against it. A child's death from a rare disease can become the rallying point for a renewed struggle against that disease. Some have suggested that the death of President John F. Kennedy's premature child from hyaline membrane disease served to renew a national search for its cure. Nationally televised news coverage of the suffering of civil rights marchers during the 1960s moved tremendous numbers of people to become involved in their struggle for justice. As much as the Holocaust revealed the awful evil that human beings are capable of perpetrating upon their brothers and sisters, it brought about some of the highest, most courageous and loving forms of human behavior as well. The entrance to Jerusalem's Yad Vashem memorial is lined with trees planted in memory of those who sheltered the fleeing Jews at great risk to their own lives. Warner Weinberg, whose child was hidden by a Dutch couple during the war, noted that

> I do not presume to know or even to speculate where God was when the gas filled the chambers in Auschwitz, when the machine-gun fire reverberated from the ledge of Babi-Yar, when live baby bodies hit the blaze of the fire pits. But I like to think that he was in the still, matter-of-fact act of deliverance performed by our Dutch couple.[25]

Finally, there is a very real sense in which it may be said that suffering can be the result of a life lived in faithful obedience to the gospel of Christ. This falls strangely upon our ears, accustomed as we are to a life of plenty. In the United States, at least, we are well past the time when the very act of committing one's life to Christ raised the specter of religious persecution. Even so, there are unpopular political and social causes to which the church is called to bring a prophetic word of judgment. Issues such as the nuclear arms race, political revolution, and sanctuary for refugees are increasingly bringing the church into opposition to the governing authorities. We have now seen prosecution of those who believe that their faith mandates a witness of resistance to governmental policies. I think of one pastor who spoke of his suffering as an offering that he could give to the God, whose presence with him enabled him to make his witness for peace. It may well be that Dietrich Bonhoeffer was correct. "We must form our estimate of [men and women] less from their achievements and failures, and more from their sufferings."[26]

We turn, then, to an examination of how the pastor

can deal with the problem of pain as it is encountered in the local church. We can theorize all we wish about approaches to the problem of suffering, but it is in the church, in the lives of those who suffer, that our theories must be put to the test.

Notes

1. Paul Tillich, *Systematic Theology*, vol. 1 (Chicago: University of Chicago Press, 1951), pp. 272ff.

2. Geddes MacGregor, *He Who Lets Us Be* (New York: Seabury Press, 1975), p. 133.

3. David R. Griffin, "Creation Out of Chaos and the Problem of Evil." In *Encountering Evil*, ed. Stephen T. Davis (Atlanta: John Knox Press, 1981), p. 101.

4. Ibid., p. 104.

5. Ibid., p. 110.

6. Daniel Day Williams, "The Vulnerable and the Invulnerable God." *Christianity and Crisis*, 22 (March 5, 1962):28.

7. David R. Griffin, "Creation Out of Chaos and the Problem of Evil," pp. 111-12.

8. John K. Roth, critique of Griffin's "Creation Out of Chaos and the Problem of Evil." In *Encountering Evil*, ed. Stephen T. Davis (Atlanta: John Knox Press, 1981), p. 119.

9. Gabriel Fackre, "Narrative Theology: An Overview." *Interpretation*, vol. 37, no. 4 (October 1983):352.

10. See John H. Hick, "An Irenaean Theodicy." In *Encountering Evil*, ed. Stephen T. Davis (Atlanta: John Knox Press, 1981), p. 122.

11. S. Paul Schilling, *God and Human Anguish* (Nashville: Abingdon Press, 1977), p. 248.

12. Leslie Weatherhead, *When the Lamp Flickers* (New York: Abingdon-Cokesbury Press, 1948), p. 141.

13. John H. Hick, *Evil and the God of Love* (San Francisco: Harper, 1978), p. 254.

14. Hick, "An Irenaean Theodicy," p. 42.

15. Ibid., p. 51.

16. Alan Paton, "Why Suffering?" In *Creative Suffering: The Ripple of Hope* (Kansas City: National Catholic Reporter Publishing Co., 1970), p. 14.

17. William Sloane Coffin, "Alex's Death." In *Sermons from Riverside*, a sermon preached at Riverside Church, New York City, on January 23, 1983, p. 2.

18. Jürgen Moltmann, *The Crucified God* (New York: Harper, 1974), p. 56.

19. Dorothee Soelle, *Suffering*, trans. Everett R. Kalin (Philadelphia: Fortress Press, 1975), p. 42.

20. Schilling, *God and Human Anguish*, pp. 248-49.

21. Some care needs to be taken as to how we express the belief that God shares our pain, lest we find ourselves in the position of feeling a need to note that God has "no nervous system." See Schilling, *God and Human Anguish*, p. 254.

22. Martin Marty, *A Cry of Absence* (San Francisco: Harper, 1983), p. 163.

23. Ronald O. Durham, "Evil and God: Has Process Made Good on Its Promise?" *Christianity Today* (June 2, 1978):14.

24. William Stringfellow, *A Simplicity of Faith*, Journeys in Faith Series, ed. Robert A. Raines (Nashville: Abingdon Press, 1982), p. 113.

25. Warner Weinberg, "A Dutch Couple." *The Christian Century* (June 22-29, 1983):615.

26. Arthur C. McGill, *Suffering*, foreword by Paul Ramsey and William F. May (Philadelphia: Westminster Press, 1982), p. 17.

Chapter Four
The Pastor's Own Vulnerability

Don't tell me Christ is risen from the dead and therefore death is a pussycat. . . . Talk me through it. And don't tell me it's silly to be angry with the surest thing in the world. I know that, but I'm still angry. So was Job. God has got to be doing something with the unending blackness of his own death and mine; otherwise, the whole thing is just a stupid arrangement which even a two-bit creator would have had the sense to straighten out.

Robert Farrar Capon, *Exit 36*

If a minister wants to be of real help in his contact with people, he has to be a professional with special information, special training, and special skills. But if he wants to break through the chains of our manipulative world, he has to move beyond professionalism, and through self-denial and contemplation, become a faithful witness of God's covenant.

Henri Nouwen, *Creative Ministry*

His name was George. He was in his late forties when he entered the hospital for some routine surgery. "Bread and butter stuff," was what he called it, referring to the fact that a major part of a general surgeon's income comes from such procedures as appendectomies, hernias, gall bladders, and so on. Neither George nor his family had any reason to suspect that there might be anything else wrong with him. My pre-surgical pastoral care of George seemed quite easy and rather routine in nature. He was to spend a few days in the hospital to recover, after which we all expected George to be back in the swing of things.

The rest of the story is well-known to many pastors. The surgeon operated on George and, in addition to the minor problem, which he repaired, he discovered a large, inoperable metastatic cancer. He was astounded that George had not experienced any pain from the disease, that he had no warning whatever that it was present.

The following day, after he had fully recovered from the grogginess of the anesthesia, George was told of the cancer. He was devastated. Later that day, I called on him. I had not been told about the cancer. I knocked at the door, entered at his invitation, and encountered an extremely angry man. There was no way to miss it. As I entered his room and he recognized me, he said, "What the hell do you want?"

DEALING WITH THE FEELINGS

Anger is one of the most common emotions encountered in persons who have learned that they are going to die sooner than they expected. It has many sources. It is born out of a sense that life is not fair, that it should contain more goodness than it often does. It derives from a feeling that one's assumed covenant with God has been breached. That anger is often directed at God's more tangible representative, the minister.

Most of us are brought up to believe that our feelings should always be carefully controlled, and none more so than anger. Anger can be violent and destructive; the damage that it does in the space of a minute can endure a lifetime.

Those of us who are on the receiving end of another person's anger experience our own conflicting feelings. Some of us, suspecting an unjustified personal attack, let our own anger come to the fore. Others of us, feeling extreme discomfort in the presence of anger, withdraw from the angry person as quickly as possible. When George vented his anger at me, either of those two responses might have made me feel easier, but would have avoided engaging George at the point of his feelings. If I had returned his anger, George would have known that I could not be trusted to help him with his angry feelings. If, on the other hand, I had retreated, saying, "Looks like this is a bad day; I'll come back tomorrow," he might fairly have assumed that I was not at all interested in his feelings or able to share them with him. Fortunately, I knew him well enough to believe that his anger could not be directed personally at me, so very quietly, I asked, "George, what happened?" With that, he became teary-eyed and told me of his cancer and of his belief that God had abandoned him.

In any theodicy related illness or death, anger is very apt to be present and needs to be expressed. It may be the product of a belief that life should contain more promise than it does. Who can disagree with that?

Psychiatrist M. Scott Peck opens his book *The Road Less Traveled*, which has become very popular, with the conviction that "life is difficult."[1] Other authors carry it further: "Life is outrageous. . . . Tragedy, pain, injustice, premature death—all of these and more waste us away."[2] In the face of this, who among us has not felt despair and anger? Of course, life is also very good, but the moment a person is struggling with the news of a terminal illness is not the time to speak of life's goodness. The message often cannot be heard.

Anger may be directly focused on God. A young mother, grappling with her infant's life-threatening illness, said, "I think God is choosy," implying that a capricious God chose to hurt her child. As pastors, we sometimes feel a need at such moments to rally to God's defense. But when we do so, we effectively close the door to further communication with the sufferer. If, on the other hand, we are free to say, "Yes, sometimes it seems like that," the door is left open.

If we approach suffering out of a conviction that the world is not perfect, that it is in the process of creation, and that God's power is not absolute, then we have little difficulty affirming the angry feelings, and providing ample opportunity for people to express them, without feeling an urgent need to defend God. If we begin with the assumption that God shares our suffering, then the angry feelings can even be seen as a way in which God works through us, expressing his own anger at life's injustice. The point is that the feelings must be allowed to come out. Dorothee Soelle wisely wrote, "If people cannot speak about their affliction they will be destroyed by it, or swallowed up by apathy."[3] If we are to minister effectively to those in pain, we must be open to their feelings, not threatened by them, and we must do all that we can to help the feelings of anger and despair to be expressed.

Another very important aspect of ministry to those who suffer has to do with examining how our own feelings and attitudes are hooked by those who suffer. This became obvious to me early in my own clinical pastoral training. As I worked with bereaved parents, I was aware that, regardless of how well I had ministered to them in their grief, no matter how often they expressed their appreciation for my help, I went away from such experiences feeling "down." Eventually, I became aware that what was being "hooked" in me were the residual feelings of loss dating back to the loss of our son. In a way, I was reliving that experience through the experience of the parents with whom I ministered. As I became aware of that dynamic within myself, I began to look for it whenever I worked with parents. Being aware of its existence and consciously working to set it aside helped it to dissipate and made me more open to the feelings of other parents, so much so that I was able to *hear* their feelings of gratitude, to accept them, and to begin to feel good about my ministry in such situations.

As we deal day by day with suffering people and experience the frustration of watching lives so filled with promise ebb away before our eyes, it is normal for us to feel a sense of despair. Often, we repress that despair under a notion that pastors must always be happy and optimistic persons. We tend to feel that we are called to bring people a word of hope, that we should never leave a patient in a state of depression. But that cannot always be the case, and we sometimes feel a sense of personal failure if we have not helped to brighten that person's day. Such a need to solve problems may lead us to aggressively reassure patients, attempt to find a solution for all of their dilemmas, and become so engrossed in our own agenda that we are no longer able to *hear* their feelings. I well remember the day, during my clinical training, when I noticed that patients were no longer bringing my conversations with them to an arbitrarily early end with comments such as, "Well, it was nice of you to come," or "Would you say a prayer for me?" At that point, I was aware of making progress at being open to their feelings, to their leading, and to their teaching. In another context, Frederick Buechner noted that the pastor is not called to be

> an actor, a magician. . . . He is called to be himself. He is called to tell the truth as he has experienced it. He is called to be human. . . . If he does not make real to them the human experience of what it is to cry into the storm and receive no answer, to be sick at heart and find no healing, then he becomes the only one there who seems not to have had that experience.[4]

How much closer we can be to suffering people when they understand that we hurt as they do and that, through our own hurt, we are open to sharing theirs.

Closely related to this is a need we may feel to always have answers to the questions people ask. The New Testament suggests that we should always be prepared to give a reason "for the hope that is within us" (I Pet. 3:15). It does not recommend that we always have to speak it. Sometimes we use words to bail ourselves out of situations in which we are not comfortable or to skirt penetrating questions we are not certain we can answer. Perhaps we fear that "to confess" our "own bewilderment"[5] is somehow to fail those to whom we would minister. Yet, to conjure up an answer that we would not dare suggest in a theology classroom serves only to make us appear foolish and does not do justice to the gospel. More often than not, the persons to whom we speak these platitudes already know that there is no answer to their question and want from us only a confirmation of that fact. How much more helpful we can be when we learn to say, "I don't know." To do so is, as David Cain says,

> neither a betrayal nor the failure of faith; to fill the emptiness with an attempt at an answer often is. To stand without answers in the presence of questions can be a way of truly hearing the questions. Faith is, among other things, the freedom *not* to know.[6]

When we erect a barrier of words between us and those whose pain we would share, we distance ourselves from their suffering and indicate to them that we are not really interested in being with them at the point of their need. Elie Wiesel, who knows more about pain than most of us, found an illustration in the story of Job and his "friends."

> These three self-righteous strangers from afar exaggerated when they tried to explain to Job events whose tragic weight rested only on his shoulders. *He* suffered, and *they* made speeches on suffering. *He* was crushed by sorrow, and *they* built theories and systems on the subjects of grief, suffering, and persecution. . . . Exasperated with his friends, Job chose to turn toward and against God. Understandably so: better to deal with God than with his commentators.[7]

When, on the other hand, we are able to admit our emptiness and frustration, acknowledge our lack of answers, and be still in the face of that which we do not understand, it is not unusual for us to find ourselves invited into a suffering person's pain. We become fellow travelers with that person on the road to light. We are standing on holy ground.

I remember an almost-two-week period during which I stood with the parents of a young child whose life was slowly ebbing away. An organ transplant had been tried in the attempt to save his life, but it had not worked. His parents and I were filled with an intense sadness at the sight of this beautiful child, slowly slipping away. The sense of gloom spread among the staff in the nursing unit, for no matter how many times nurses have seen death, the death of a child touches them at a deeper level of frustration.

Over the course of the days, I had shared with the parents my own sense of frustration, my experience of losing our son and the futility that I felt in connection with it, and my sense of the injustice of their child's illness. Over the days, we prayed for a miracle for them, but it was not to be. There were many tears when the child died, including the nurses' and my own. Shortly before the parents left the hospital for home, the mother said to me, "It must be terribly difficult for you [chaplains] to be in situations like this and know that there is nothing that can be done and know that there aren't any answers. But I want you to know that you've been a tremendous support to both of us." Holy ground.

However, assuming that we have been able to hear and to share the feelings of those to whom we minister, at what point, then, do we speak? And about what? There are ample pastoral counseling texts and clinical experiences to train pastors for ministry with the terminally ill, but one area in particular seems to need emphasis: the pastor's own experience with suffering.

It is often said that pastors should avoid talking about their own experiences. There are times when this is good advice, but not always.

One day, as I was working in my office at the church, the telephone rang. On the other end was a physician on the neo-natal intensive care staff at our local hospital. He told me of a young couple whose infant daughter was near death and who had no pastoral affiliation. I had worked with this doctor before, and he was aware of my own experience of loss. So after getting permission from the parents, he called me. I met with them in the room adjoining their daughter's room, the room in which they had been living ever since their daughter became ill. We were complete strangers to each other and, as I listened to them speak of their love for their daughter and of her impending death, I found myself reliving my own experience of loss once again. When it seemed appropriate, I shared that experience with them and, though strangers, we finished our conversation standing with our arms around one another, united in a common understanding, a common pain.

The death of a child appears for all the world to be an experience that will completely overwhelm us, so great is the grief. There is a very real fear that we will not have the resources to deal with it. Like David, we exhaust ourselves with hoping and praying (II Sam. 12:16-17). It can be of real help to us to share that load with someone else whose life has been marked by such an experience. Henri Nouwen has written of the wounded healer whose service "will not be perceived as authentic unless it comes from a heart wounded by the suffering about which he speaks."[8]

There will always be those well-meaning souls who come to call, like Job's friends, with no real understanding of pain and with their own agenda for dealing with it. My wife can well remember being called upon in the hospital by a group of people who insisted on praying for her without regard for her needs or feelings. Unfortunately, such events are not as rare as one might hope, and many hospitals have been forced to screen visitors to protect patients from those whose aim is not so much to bring help as it is to proselytize.

There are others who, having had just the slightest brush with illness in their lives, yet feel that they have earned the right to claim understanding of virtually anyone's pain. There have been pastors who have said, "I know how hard this must be for you," only to have a patient respond with a well-deserved "No, you don't." While the sharing of pain can help to bring pastor and patient together, great care must be exercised in such sharing. Nouwen is right:

> Making one's wounds a source of healing . . . does not call for a sharing of superficial personal pains but for a constant willingness to see one's own pain and suffering as rising from the depth of the human condition which all [persons] share.[9]

In a very real sense, pastors must become vulnerable, both in reliving their own pain and in accepting and sharing the pain of those with whom they are in ministry. One of the church's hymns speaks of how

We share each other's woes,
Our mutual burdens bear,
And often for each other flows,
The sympathizing tear.
("Blest Be the Tie That Binds")

As we minister in this way, sharing each other's pain, we incarnate our faith in the God who stands with us in our suffering, sharing its burden. It is a ministry of vulnerability.

PASTORAL VULNERABILITY

To speak of vulnerability is to suggest that a caring pastor relates to a dying parishioner in a different manner than do many of the other health care professionals surrounding the patient. A patient is encircled by social workers, laboratory technicians, radiologists, dieticians, nurses, and physicians. Each of them has a carefully designated specialty, whose role is clearly defined in the health care delivery system.

The part played by the pastor in the healing process is much less clearly defined and has been a source of confusion and personal struggle for many pastors. I think of a conversation that I had with a newly appointed hospital chaplain, in which he shared his personal struggle with trying to define and claim his own authority in the hospital setting. All around him were professionals who seemed to know exactly what they were doing and what part their activity played in the healing process. "They know what they are doing and can measure its success," he said. "The patient either gets well or does not. But how do I measure what I do?" Because the role played by spiritual resources

89

often seems so intangible, pastors may feel a sense of inadequacy.

The sense of inadequacy has tempted some pastors to take on the characteristics of their co-workers. They have tried to become amateur physicians or novice psychiatrists. It seems to lend a sense of authenticity when one can speak knowingly of such mysteries as obsessive-compulsive disorders, chronic obstructive pulmonary disease, anticipatory grief, or intra-venous infiltration.

There *is* a need for us to be as informed as we possibly can with regard to what takes place around us in the hospital. We *do* need to know what our fellow healers are doing and what role is being played by their activity. But that knowledge should be used as a means of helping us to relate our own specialty to the patient's well being, not as a means of helping us to imitate the activity of other professionals.

Henri Nouwen has called us to account, wondering if we "have not become more immersed in the language of the behavioral sciences than in the language of the Bible."[10] Jacques Ellul has raised the question as to whether it is as psychoanalysts that pastors would rather "act in the Christian community."[11]

To some degree, this situation has come about as a result of what seemed to some pastors a denigration of their profession by other health care providers with whom they worked. Fortunately, as the healing of persons has come to be seen in holistic terms, more caregivers have recognized the unique roles played by all, including the pastor. No one is better prepared to speak to the theological concerns raised by those who suffer. No one is better equipped to speak to the questions of faith, grace, life, death, and resurrection than the pastor. As Paul Pruyser has noted, when a person comes to the pastor and "raises a theological question," that person has "knocked at the right door."[12] The pastor brings special resources to bear in achieving the healing of body and spirit.

USE AND MISUSE OF PRAYER

One of those resources is prayer. It is a most powerful tool and requires care in its use. We may pray with a person only to discover later that the prayer was interpreted to mean that he or she was sicker than she or he really knew! Prayer can be very cathartic for a frightened patient. In my experience, it has been very common to see prayer move people to tears and free them to share anxious feelings.

It is possible to abuse prayer. Struggling with our own agendas, wishing that a talkative patient would realize that we have other people to visit, we may aggressively suggest, "Well, why don't we share a prayer together, and then I'll see you tomorrow!" Not only have we rejected a patient's need to be heard, but we have also violated one of the purposes of prayer, the summing up of feelings and the offering of those feelings to God.

It is also possible to abuse prayer by making it a means of saying what the patient has refused to say. Once again, our agenda gets in the way. We hear a patient say that there is always hope, even though we see little basis for it, and we wish the patient would come to grips with the fact—so plain to us—that he or she is going to die. We have a need to help a patient move through the stages of dying, from anger to acceptance, just as all the textbooks seem to say the patient should. And so, out of *our* need, not the patient's, we speak in *our* prayer of imminent death. We go away from the patient, feeling that we have achieved something, when possibly all that we have accomplished is to create uneasiness or fear. One counselor, Daniel C. DeArment, has written meaningfully about pastors who misuse prayer: "as a way of violating the patient's defenses, making him feel that the office of the ministry and the power of God have stripped away what conventional good manners, changes of subject, and other defenses could effectively keep covered."[13] In cases such as this, the pastor should not be surprised when, upon returning to see the patient again, he or she finds a sign attached to the door: "Visitors, please stop at the nursing station before seeing the patient!"

Another problem that we may experience in the use of prayer is that of seeing it as a means of avoiding a subject that we would rather not confront in our conversation with the patient. Again, it is our own feelings, our own agenda, that gets in the way of communication. If a pastor has not come to terms with death and mortality, it can be very difficult for her or him to speak of death with a terminally ill patient. It is easy to say, "Oh, you're not going to die," denying what everyone else—including the patient—believes to be true. That discomfort may even move us to bring the conversation to a close with the suggestion of prayer. In doing so, we have used prayer to deny the patient the opportunity to talk through her or his own fears of dying.

Over the course of my ministry, I have learned much from patients and counselors about the use of prayer with those who are suffering. I have made it a habit to visit with patients on the afternoon or evening before they are to have surgery. If the surgery is particularly critical in nature, I try to be with them during the time immediately before they are taken to the operating room and, if possible, I like to remain with the patient's family during the tense hours of waiting to learn of the outcome. Prayer at such times can serve to buoy up the patient and his or her family. In order not to worry the patient, I have learned to say that I *routinely* like to share prayer with *everyone* before surgery and then *ask* the patient's permission to do this. Most of the time, a patient is eager to have me pray. On rare occasions, however, when a person indicates that he or she would rather not have me pray, it is important to respect that decision. For all we know, the hospital chaplain may have visited prior to our coming and may have offered prayer and left the patient feeling quite well. When a patient rejects an offer of prayer, there is no personal rejection necessarily involved. People facing surgery have enough on their minds without our adding to their worry by pressing a prayer upon them. Again, it is a matter of whose needs are being served.

The content of our prayers is also important. I try to include the fears that have surfaced during my conversation with the patient, the questions that have been raised, the uncertainty that is evident. On occasion, when I feel a genuine fear just below the surface of the patient's words, I will lift that up as well. But great care must be taken to avoid saying what the

93

patient does not want said. It is not uncommon for such prayer to aid patients in releasing their fear, thus playing a therapeutic role in their healing.

One question that seems to surface often at this point is what to pray about. "When I know that my parishioner is going to die, what do I pray for?" Many dynamics are at work here. There are, not least of all, the pastor's own questions about the efficacy of prayer. If everyone, including the patient, knows that death is imminent, what sense does it make to pray for healing? There is also the pastor's need to be helpful to the patient. There is the possibility of guilt experienced after saying the wrong thing. There are the ever-present hopes of the sufferer and family for a miracle of healing to take place. If, as is often the case toward the end of a terminal illness, the patient is comatose, what should be said?

In circumstances such as these, a loving pastor feels severely tested. But there are meaningful things that can be done. We now believe that even comatose persons seem to be able to hear what we have to say.[14] If death seems imminent, it is entirely appropriate to pray for God's support in time of pain, for help in trusting God's care, for belief that God shares our suffering with us, and to express our thanks that God is with the person that we love, helping that person to know that she or he is not alone. When death is very near, I have found the old benediction from Numbers 6:25-26 to be meaningful:

The Lord bless you and keep you:
The Lord make his face to shine
   upon you, and be gracious to
   you:
The Lord lift up his countenance
   upon you, and give you peace.

One of the most meaningful points in our ministry at which prayer can be used effectively is following the death of a patient. It can express our thanks to God for the life and love of the person who has died, thereby summing up feelings that nearby relatives want to share but may feel reluctant to voice in the awkwardness of the moment. I like to have the relatives join hands with me around the side of the patient's bed. A prayer with them can commend the care of the person to God and ask for help for those who remain, assisting them in putting their trust in God as well. Again, relying on our understanding that God knows and shares our pain, the prayer can express that faith. Where the death has left us with many unanswered and frustrating questions, we may share those questions with God. It is helpful to those who remain to know that it is appropriate to share even feelings of bitterness and confusion with God, always, however, accompanied by a reminder that God understands our despair, has felt it, and will use our trust to support our struggle to heal.

Often, prayer after a death provides the break needed by family members to return to their homes and give over the care of the remains to the hospital staff and funeral home. On one occasion recently, the room of a child who had died was filled not only with relatives, but also with hospital staff people who had struggled to preserve the life of the baby. Their grief was as real as that of the parents. When that happens, a final prayer can express our thanks to God for those who have worked so hard and given so much of themselves on behalf of the one who has died. These persons had been an important part of the life of the deceased and his or her family; they should not be left out at the end of the struggle.

It should be obvious by now that the major task of the pastor in ministry to the terminally ill is that of being sensitively present, listening to and interpreting their anxieties, helping them give voice to their feelings, being a theological resource when it is appropriate, and when possible, helping the sufferer move to a point of accepting illness and placing trust in God. It has been called a ministry of "being-with" persons at this most important moment in their lives.[15] It is a sacred journey that is entrusted to a faithful pastor by a suffering person. Henri Nouwen's words are apt: "Sorrow is an unwelcome companion and . . . anyone who willingly enters into the pain of a stranger is truly a remarkable person."[16]

Notes

1. M. Scott Peck, *The Road Less Traveled* (New York: Simon and Schuster, 1978), p. 15.

2. John K. Roth, "A Theodicy of Protest." In *Encountering Evil,* ed. Stephen T. Davis (Atlanta: John Knox Press, 1981), p. 20

3. Dorothee Soelle, *Suffering,* trans. Everett R. Kalin (Philadelphia: Fortress Press, 1975), p. 76.

4. Frederick Buechner, *Telling the Truth* (San Francisco: Harper, 1977), p. 40.

5. D. W. Cleverly Ford, *The Ministry of the Word* (Grand Rapids, Mich.: Eerdman's, 1979), pp. 146-47.

6. David Cain, "A Way of God's Theodicy: Honesty, Presence, Adventure." *The Journal of Pastoral Care,* 32 (December 1978):241.

7. Elie Wiesel, *Messengers of God* (New York: Random House, 1976), pp. 225-26.

8. Henri Nouwen, *The Wounded Healer* (New York: Doubleday Image Books, 1979), p. xvi.

9. Ibid., p. 88.

10. Henri Nouwen, *The Living Reminder* (New York: Seabury Press, 1977), p. 24.

11. Jacques Ellul, *The Ethics of Freedom,* ed. and trans. Geoffrey W. Bromiley (Grand Rapids, Mich.: Eerdman's, 1976), p. 503.

12. Paul Pruyser, *The Minister as Diagnostician* (Philadelphia: Westminster Press, 1976), p. 48.

13. Daniel C. DeArment, "Prayer and the Dying Patient: Intimacy Without Exposure." In *Death and Ministry,* eds. J. Donald Bane et al. (New York: Seabury Press, 1977), pp. 56-57.

14. See, for example, Alquinn L. Toews, "A Ministry to the

Unconscious Patient." In *Pastor and Patient,* ed. Richard Dayringer (New York: Jason Aaronson, 1981), pp. 179-83.

15. See, for example, Carleton J. Sweetser, "The Bereaved in the Hospital." In *Death and Ministry,* cited above, and Liston O. Mills, *Perspectives on Death* (New York: Abingdon Press, 1969), pp. 253-83.

16. Henri Nouwen, *In Memoriam* (Notre Dame, Ind.: Ave Maria Press, 1980), p. 14.

Chapter Five
Light in the Presence of Darkness

Facing death means facing the ultimate questions of the meaning of life. If we really want to live we must have the courage to recognize that life is ultimately very short, and that everything we do counts. When it is the evening of our life we will hopefully have a chance to look back and say: "It was worthwhile because I have really lived."

Elisabeth Kübler-Ross, *Death: The Final Stage of Growth*

You speak of God, and I—Sometimes, at church, I hear the priest describe the Lord's suffering—and I wonder whether the Lord isn't suffering because He must listen to sermons.

Elie Wiesel, *The Trial of God*

Death is swallowed up in victory. (I Corinthians 15:54b)

His name was Brent. It was a hot and humid day when the call came from the funeral home. Brent had been with a group of his friends, taking advantage of the nearby river to relieve the heat of the mid-July sun. It was a place where they had gone swimming for several years. Not one of the parents worried about their swimming in the river. We never knew just what happened, but for some reason, when Brent swung out over the water on a rope and let go, he never came up. It was something that the boys had done for years without difficulty. The water had been running a little high for that time of the year. The current may have washed some obstacle into the swimming hole that the boys were unable to see. The attempts at explanation seemed almost endless, but the result remained unchanged: Brent was gone. The accident hit me particularly hard. I had just confirmed Brent that spring.

The call came, as it often does, from the funeral director rather than the parents. I immediately drove out to their farm, finding it hard to believe that the bright, articulate young man whom I had enjoyed in confirmation class was gone. As is so often the case when death comes suddenly, unexpectedly, Brent's parents were in a state of confusion and shock. There was disbelief: "How could this have happened to Brent?" Deep bitterness was directed at God: "Why didn't God help Brent?" There was great uncertainty as to what needed to be done: "What do we have to do about the funeral?"

I went about the task of ministering to them as best I knew how. As for how it could have happened, I had no better answers than they did. All I could do was to share my own feelings of grief. As for whether or not God could let it happen to their son, I urged them to express as much anger as they wanted; it was not the time to rally to God's defense. As for the business of preparing for the funeral, I offered to go with them to meet with the funeral director and help them make the arrangements. In preparing for the memorial service, I shared with them my understanding of death and how I saw it in the total context of God's gift of life. We talked at length about their son. I urged them to share with me their significant memories of him, as I took notes for the sermon that I would prepare later. I ended my visit with a prayer, sharing our frustrations and anger, our questions, and our feeling of abandonment and closed by commending Brent's life to God's care.

The following morning, I met the parents at the funeral home to help them make the arrangements. Matters can become awkward at this point. Out of my understanding of resurrection's emphasis on a spiritual body that is God's gift to us after death and the perishable nature of our physical body, as Paul wrote in I Corinthians 15, I urged them not to spend an exorbitant amount of money. Such advice may conflict with a feeling on the part of the bereaved that the funeral offers to them their last opportunity to do as much as they can for the deceased. No such conflict arose on that occasion, and we were able to complete the arrangements with as little pain as possible.

Brent's funeral was held, not at the funeral home, but at the church. The presence of organ and hymnals enabled everyone to take part in the service, singing the praise of the God who came to us in Jesus Christ and gave to us the promise of a new life. The funeral went well, providing an ending point for the family's relationship with Brent and getting them started at the task of picking up the pieces of their lives. One week later, I called on them again, helping them to continue to release their feelings, urging them to continue to cry whenever they felt the need. At intervals of two weeks

101

to a month, I continued to call on them until I sensed that they had completed their grieving and were well on the road to living with Brent's memory. One final call, many months later, completed my pastoral care. On Brent's birthday—a day I knew would be particularly difficult for them—I dropped in again to visit and share a prayer with them. On that occasion, they showed me the large photograph of Brent they had placed in their living room. Surrounding it in the frame was a copy of the sermon I had preached at Brent's memorial service. I left them that day with a deep sense of having been a part of their healing.

Whether lay or clergy, whether through memorial address or an embrace of support, we love most deeply when we attempt to bring healing to those caught up in pain. Never is that more true than when suffering has brought an end to the life of a loved one. There, where the need is the greatest, however, we often stand tongue-tied in the face of the mystery. How many times have we heard, "I just didn't know what to say." But there are words that can be spoken, words that can bring light into the darkness of suffering and death.

Working from our understanding of the problem of evil, as developed in the earlier chapters, we can proclaim the gospel in a way in which we affirm our human worth in the sight of God, in which we are not left alone in the presence of suffering and death, and in which God actively shares our grief.

Whether we speak the words in Sunday worship or a memorial service, our sermons must be marked by a direct confronting of the questions raised by suffering and death. We dare not duck the questions if what we say is to have any reality at all. The temptation to try to answer all of the questions must be avoided. As Nathan Scott wrote, the pastor can seem to be "in so great a hurry to resolve enigma as to claim to know more than he really does."[1] To attempt to appear as if we have the inside track on all the answers can make us appear ignorant and insensitive to the reality of the mourner's pain. At the same time, though, it is essential that it be evident that we have also wrestled with the enigma. As has been indicated, there is no shame in admitting our own sense of anger and lack of answers. Indeed, without such an admission, our credibility may suffer greatly. "When words try to sneak up on suffering, they easily sound tinny."[2]

With those considerations of the sermon in mind, and building upon the theological understanding of suffering from the earlier chapters, I would like to suggest a number of approaches to preaching that can be of help to those who are struggling with this problem. Nathan Scott reminds us that

> of all the myriad issues of life which the Christian pulpit is required to handle there is none so pressing, so inescapable, and so burdensome for the preacher as the problem of suffering, the mystery of iniquity, the strange and brutal haphazardness with which as it seems at time, acute misfortune is distributed amongst persons.[3]

Whatever the context, treating the problem of pain is one of the heaviest responsibilities that we will ever face in the course of our pastoral ministry.

ALLOWING THE QUESTIONS TO SPEAK

When a person who is well up in years comes to the end of life, unless death has been accompanied by great

103

suffering, we seldom find that death to be the cause for raising questions of God's goodness. When an adolescent of thirteen dies suddenly, unexpectedly, questions abound. Why did God let this happen? Where was God when the teenager died? Doesn't God care about his children? Those are just a few of the more common questions that spring out of the grief. It is terribly important that there be no attempt on the part of the pastor to prevent these questions from being asked and precipitously attempting to defend the goodness of God. Questions about the goodness of God spring out of deep feelings of anger and alienation. These feelings must be allowed expression if a broken spirit is to begin to heal.

One of the reasons for such questioning has to do with the popular belief, discussed previously, that our faith should somehow protect us from harm. David H. C. Read, referring to the parable of the prodigal son, suggests that

> in spite of hearing innumerable sermons on the grace of God and receiving the sacrament of Holy Communion in which it is made evident that "Nothing is my hand I bring, simply to thy cross I cling," average churchgoers . . . are not content to be prodigal sons . . . but see themselves rather as elder brothers with some claim on the Father for their years of service.[4]

Like the elder brother in the parable, some folks feel that because they have served faithfully they should be taken care of and protected by God. Certainly, that idea is heavily embedded in our cultural religion. We need only flip the television dial to virtually the nearest television evangelist to discover that faith and well-being seem to be heavily tied together. Many of us grow up believing that hard work promises success, and it is but a short step from that understanding to a belief that faith should do the same. Time and time again, as I have been with grieving people in the hospital, I have heard that sentiment expressed. "Why has this happened to me? I've never hurt anyone" is one form of the question. There is also a reverse side to the question: "The fellow who lives down the street from me never goes to church and has never helped anyone in his life; yet, he never seems to have any troubles at all. If having faith doesn't protect you, then why bother with it?"

Rather than pointing up the poor theological understanding contained in such questions, one should treat them as an opportunity. Edgar Jackson, an authority on the subject of grief, noted that our "questions represent the growing edge" of our lives.[5] When such questions are asked of a pastor by a suffering or dying parishioner, they can become the means by which the pastor begins to express an understanding of the problem upon which the parishioner can build a more hopeful faith.

I have noted above my conviction that the way in which the pastor accepts or rejects such questions may determine whether a parishioner will come to trust the pastor enough to share the real feelings of fear and loneliness, which are beyond the questions. As John R. Cobb wrote:

> The question, Why me? cannot be given a theological answer. But the pastor can explain why there is cancer in the world and how God intends that we respond to it. . . . We can believe that the death which this cancer will bring is not the end of life but only the transition to other lives, that eventually we will all be perfected.[6]

105

There are many occasions when it seems entirely appropriate to raise the "why" questions themselves in a sermon, even if they have not previously been raised by the mourners. It is a safe assumption that the questions are present in the minds of the congregation. Their being raised in the sermon indicates a willingness to confront the thorny issues, builds a sense of empathy with the mourners, and increases the intensity with which the congregants listen to what is being said. One can see the heads nod in agreement, and the eyes of the congregation become more intensely fixed on the pulpit.

Does that mean that we must be able to answer all of the questions that are raised? Obviously not. As already indicated, there is great value in the pastor's being secure enough to admit that he or she has also struggled with the uncertainty. It has been my experience that this kind of honesty often results in persons' being able to feel that the pastor knows where they are hurting and shares their feelings. It serves to open the door to further communication.

Simply voicing the questions, however, is not all that needs to be done. The questions should be turned in the direction of the healing that the gospel can give to those who seek it. Rabbi Jacob Philip Rudin, writing out of the experience of having lost his wife, suggests that "why" questions be turned in the direction of "where" questions. Instead of asking "Why did God let it happen?" there is more hope to be found in asking, "Where was God when it happened?" Once having turned in search of God's presence, he was able to come to believe that "God was in the quiet gratitude of her joys. He was in the victory of her courage. He was . . . in her humor, which never forsook her."[7] Building on an interpretation that finds God a part of our lives, sharing our suffering and taking it upon himself, we are more able to discover the presence of God in other aspects of the life of a dying person. Even when answers are difficult to find, to know that God is present serves to ease the fear of many. Edmund Steimle has noted that "this is precisely how God showed his mighty power in a cross and Resurrection. We are never given an explanation, but an assurance of a presence."[8]

Another way in which the "why" questions can be turned in the direction of healing builds on the process element in our view of the problem of pain. If we can accept the belief that the world is still in the process of creation and that we are also involved in a process of becoming, then suffering and death can be viewed not as the end of everything, but rather as a summons to us by the God who shares our pain to transform suffering and death into a creative force. It need not be "allowed to build up into a dark patch of loveless resentment and meaningless futility."[9] Holding before the congregation a view of the cross transformed through the resurrection shows the effect that it had upon the disciples and demonstrates the possibility of accepting suffering and death and learning to minister even in the face of pain. Paul did just this, noting in Romans 8 that "The sufferings of this present time are not worth comparing with the glory that is to be revealed to us. . . . We know that in everything God works for good with those who love him" (8:18, 28). One can also recall the experience of Job as he gave vent to all of the questions that plagued him. The more we enable the questions to be expressed, the more we help others to

107

see that, while we may not escape suffering and death, we are given a Presence in the midst of our despair, which enables us to endure and to overcome. It is in this direction that the sermon should move in the treatment of the questions that are always present in the midst of unexplained suffering and death.

THE INEVITABILITY OF DEATH

Preaching should present the inevitability of death. To varying degrees, shock is felt in every confrontation with death, but never more than when the death seems unexpected, unjust, or involves someone quite young. The shock produces a numbing kind of disbelief. Though everyone knows that death is a part of life, it is not something we readily discuss or consider.

The Bible, on the other hand, is matter of fact in its acceptance of the inevitability of death. The preacher notes that "For everything there is a season," that there is "a time to be born, and a time to die" (Eccles. 3:1a, 2a). We are less quick to accept that, however.

While the death of a child or middle-aged parent may leave us with a deep sense of injustice, it is the responsibility of the pastor to gently and compassionately set that death in context. It is the understanding that death is a reality facing all of us that leads us to accept it and to learn to pour all of ourselves into each day of our lives. Following such a reminder in a Sunday sermon, a busy insurance executive in one of my congregations vowed to stop going in to the office on Saturdays and to spend more time with his children.

Martin Marty describes this in a beautiful way in his book *A Cry of Absence,* noting that

> in various ways all people are on a terminal course. Cells in the body move toward their inevitable end. Yet while they threaten . . . the death of the body, the people in whom they work read poetry, welcome psalms, make love, enjoy the cup and the table, and bask in friendship.[10]

Death is a part of life. More than the end of life, it should be seen as a constant part of our experience. When a person retires from a job that has contributed meaning to his or her life and to his or her sense of self worth, a little dying takes place. When families or friends move away—almost the rule rather than the exception in today's mobile society—something of our sense of having roots dies along with the move. We have learned to live with the death of love in a time when almost half of all marriages end in divorce.

Our preaching should take seriously this omnipresence of death-like changes in our society. We need to be about the business of searching for forms of meaningful living within this context of movement and change. The God whom we worship in Jesus Christ is a wanderer, moving into the wilderness with Abraham, leading the Israelites from bondage into the Promised Land, accompanying them into exile in Babylon. He is a God ever-free, ever-changing, ever-present. In every "valley of the shadow" we have heard his voice: "Comfort, comfort my people" (Isa. 41:1).

It is through coming to understand death's presence in our lives in so many little ways that we are enabled to come to terms with our ultimate dying. Yet, even at that moment, the voice of God is present. "I will not leave you desolate; I will come to you" (John 14:18).

As we face the death of a child, we cannot sound too strongly this note of God's presence. In the midst of their grief at losing their son or daughter, there is in the parents a deep need for assurance that all is well with their child. It is our nature as parents to want to protect our children from harm. When we are unable to do this, when our children are beyond the reach of our arms, we need to know that God is protecting them for us.

There is a need on the part of the parents to know that in time their hurt will ease, that they will be able to go on with their living. When a child dies, everything seems to come to an end. If children, with all of their freshness and promise and innocence, can die with no apparent reason, then all of life seems to be called into question.

Yet, the God of our faith also experienced the death of his son, has felt our anguish, and will help us to bear the pain and absurdity of it all. When we are faithful in proclaiming this word of hope, when we can come to see that, while death is ever-present, we are not alone, then death loses some of its threat. The late William Stringfellow said it well: "Paradoxically, it is when a human being can be said to be most authentically alive that that person becomes free to die imminently or at any moment."[11]

Death is a part of life. It comes to some soon, to others later, but it comes. Though it seems such, it is no alien intruder, crashing in upon us from outside our experience. We must learn to come to terms with it long before the end of life. Preaching can help us do that.

THE IMPORTANCE OF EACH DAY

Closely related to the presentation of death's inevitability is preaching's theme of living to the fullest each and every day. Jesus reminds us to "Take no thought for the morrow" (Matt 6:34), but we continue to live as if there will never be an ending to it all. We save for "rainy days," plan a special trip "when the kids are grown," and postpone meaningful experiences "until our ship comes in." When, suddenly, we are forced to confront the death of someone we love, well before the time that we may have expected it, we discover that the "rainy day" is now.

I have been preaching this theme off and on for some years now and recently had cause to be glad for that preaching. A young husband who unexpectedly lost his wife to cancer found tremendous consolation in remembering the "dream" trip that they had taken together. They had put it off and put it off until one Sunday in church they heard a sermon, urging the congregation to take advantage of each day. They went home, had dinner together, talked about the sermon, and decided to take the "dream" vacation they had been postponing for years. The trip was, for them, a kind of re-creation of the feelings they held for each other early in their marriage. They loved every minute of the vacation. A year later, she was dead. As her husband cast about in his mind for meaning, it was that sermon and that trip that came back in his collection of memories, bringing with it a feeling of consolation.

There is no way to put a value on the little things we do each day. They seem small at the time, but they return in a time of death as sources of comfort. The time we take to talk with a child at bedtime, the hugs that we share, the tender touch, an encouraging word, all take on tremendous significance in a time of pain. Elisabeth Kübler-Ross came to this understanding out of her research with dying patients, realizing that

> you live your life in preparation for tomorrow or in remembrance of yesterday, and meanwhile, each today is lost. In contrast, when you fully understand that each day you awaken could be the last day that you have, you take the time *that day* to grow, to become more of who you really are, to reach out to other human beings.[12]

The psalmist prayed, "teach us to number our days" (90:12), and we must help ourselves and others to do so. It is part of our responsibility as pastors to help persons hear the gospel's urgency and to incarnate it in their family life. When we stand in the pulpit, looking at the anguish of someone who has lost a loved one prematurely, it is of great help to recall the little moments in which that person lived fully and meaningfully.

SPEAKING OF GOD

During the later years of my seminary career, two theological/philosophical movements—logical positivism and linguistic analysis—were very popular. Of great concern to proponents of these movements was the matter of how God is spoken about in a logical manner. When we confront the problem of suffering, especially when that suffering has led to the death of someone we love, how we speak about God is of supreme importance.

In many ways, the entire first section of this volume has been preparation for this, but more needs to be said. In the face of tragedy, probably the most difficult problem facing the pastor who must prepare for the memorial service is the question, "What can I say about God that will have any meaning at a time like this?" In a context marked by doubt about God's goodness and questions about God's power, we tend to feel like the psalmist who, in his despair, asked: "How shall we sing the Lord's song in a foreign land?" (137:4).

We have spoken of the insensitivity of the pastor who rushes in to answer all of these questions prematurely when the questions are but the mantle that covers feelings of anger and despair in the bereaved. Kübler-Ross reminds us that it is "inappropriate to speak of the love of God"[13] in such a context. It is equally inappropriate to rush to God's defense. It is tempting to do so since, whether rightly or wrongly, we tend to see ourselves in the role of spokespersons for the eternal. But, once again, such an attempt to prevent doubts from being raised makes us appear to have no appreciation for the very real pain that is being felt by the bereaved. The frustration that this can create on the part of those who have been hurt is admirably expressed in a letter by a former patient to her hospital chaplain. "Oh glory to skip the how-are-you-fines sometime and hear you say *hell* from the heart![14]

Sooner or later, however, the time comes for us to begin to set tragedy in the light of the gospel. Assuming that we have acknowledged the presence of doubt and the feelings of alienation that accompany it, we can

113

begin to move meaningfully toward an interpretation that can facilitate healing.

Once again we begin by coming to grips with the popular belief that faith in God should protect us from all of life's vicissitudes. As Edmund Steimle noted:

> Every temptation our Lord had to meet was in one way or another a temptation to escape suffering and death. Yet we continue to think of God's power almost exclusively in those terms. Of course it's understandable. . . . But the strange answer from the New Testament is not "I will save you from these things," but "Lo, I am with you always, even to the end of the age."[15]

Earlier, I spoke of my conviction that God is present with us and shares the suffering and death that we experience. Although the psalmist struggled with the call to sing the Lord's song in an alien environment, it was the Hebrews' conviction that God went into exile with them that sustained them and gave them hope for a return to Israel. When Roman persecution decimated the ranks of the early Christians, it was their conviction that God shared their suffering and triumphed over it that kept their hopes alive.

Dorothee Soelle reminds us that our faith has two central elements, "the dark night of despair, the cross on which we are hammered without being asked," and the resurrection, which reminds us of the "unending affirmation of life that arises in the dark night of the cross."[16] These are the elements that should form the core of our preaching about God in the face of tragedy. God has been there with us, understanding our feelings, providing us with hope of life beyond the grave, and sustaining us as we begin to rebuild our lives. Edgar N. Jackson, examining the help that faith provides to those who mourn, wrote that faith should help a person "find the resources in the history and experience of man that fortify his understanding and give him a sense of the changeless in the midst of change, of the eternal in the midst of time," and enable us to gather "up the tragic" and transform "it by the direction of its hope and the power of its love."[17]

While all of these things can be said of the suffering and death of those we love, there is also a message present for those who remain. The sermon should also serve to remind its hearers that we need not wait for the time of our ultimate death to experience the presence of God, but that this can be present reality for us as well. Jesus spoke of the need for his followers to "take up the cross and follow me" in the knowledge that "whoever loses his life for my sake will find it" (Matt. 16:24-25).

Out of her belief that Christianity is "the religion of the oppressed, of those marked by affliction," Dorothee Soelle wrote that "Christianity sees life better preserved by those who have died once."[18] The late theologian William Stringfellow, whose own life knew its share of suffering, wrote poignantly of the death of his close friend, Anthony Towne. Stringfellow expressed his belief that

> having already died in Christ, [Towne's] selfhood had been rescued, established, identified, fulfilled, and finished, so that his death, while poignant, was not waste or tragedy or demonic triumph or incentive to despair. . . . Anthony had found his life in his loss of life in Christ.[19]

The call to give up our lives to Christ and the assurance that we will receive them back again is not often heard in memorial sermons. It should properly be there. It is the way in which we are able to help persons prepare for their own time of suffering and death.

THE NEED FOR MEANING

Of all the problems created by the mystery of suffering, none strikes us as deeply as our need for an assurance of meaning. When a child dies, it seems as if its birth was meaningless. It is common to hear anguished parents ask: "If she was only to live for a few months, why in the world was she born? Where's the sense in it?" As pastors, we know that every life is precious in the sight of God, regardless of its length, but this is less evident to those who know only the pain of losing their son or daughter.

The same sort of question occurs when death prematurely claims a young adult. What with modern medicine's continual lengthening of our life-span, when death takes a young man or woman right at the peak of life's promise, we search again for some sense of meaning to such a loss, all the more so when death leaves young children without a parent.

As difficult as it seems to be, it is possible for pastors to find meaning in these situations and, in so doing, to bring their faith to bear upon the reality of death. That can be one factor that provides hope for those who mourn, until such time as mourning eases, and they are really able to hear the gospel's promise.

Assuming that we have treated sensitively the feelings and questions that were noted above, we need then to examine the question of longevity. There is no doubt that when death claims someone in the prime of life it arouses in us a sense of injustice. We expect persons to live long enough to retire and to be able to enjoy that life past their sixties. There are some who, having heard the psalmist's formula of "threescore and ten" (90:10), take that as a kind of benchmark. But our understanding of the problem of suffering reminds us of the randomness of pain, that it strikes good as well as evil, young as well as old, and that God is not its author. As a rabbi wrote:

> God must not be reduced to a cosmic Book-keeper Who doles out the years, so many to one person, so many to another. His justice is not to be reckoned in terms of His generosity with years bestowed. . . . God is not in the measurement nor in the comparison of life with life, reward with reward, blessing with blessing, hard death or easy death.[20]

To believe that God is responsible for a premature death is to raise again the specter of a capricious deity. It makes of God one who deserves our anger more than our adoration.

The God in whom we place our faith is rather the God whose Son was crucified, fully experiencing the suffering that plagues us. He is a God who shares our pain and aloneness, who takes it upon himself and is deeply a part of our search for meaning. Just as new life issued from the death of Christ, so also there are ways in which life can be found in the darkest recesses of our pain if, through the eyes of faith, we look for them.

Harold S. Kushner, writing in the aftermath of his son's death, realized that "I am a more sensitive person, a more effective pastor, a more sympathetic counselor because of Aaron's life and death than I would ever have been without it."[21] I can affirm his

117

belief through my own experience. In the loss of my son, resources for ministry have been given to me that I could have found in no other way. Every time I enter the presence of parents grieving at the loss of a child, it is with a sense of knowing how they are feeling and with a belief that I am better equipped to help them deal with the pain. Like Kushner, I would gladly trade those benefits if it meant that my son might be returned to me, but that is not one of the options I face. I must deal with reality, not wishes, and the reality is that I can find meaning in the short time that my wife's and my lives were enriched by Kent's having been a part of them.

Less than a year after our loss, I was called to deliver the memorial sermon at a service for the baby of a couple to whom we were very close. After the committal service, the child's father said, "I wouldn't have ever believed that anything could make me feel hopeful after what we've been through, but after that service, at least I'm willing to try." I don't think we can ask for any better affirmation of our ministry than that.

In every sermon in which I have tried to lift up elements of meaning that may not have otherwise been seen, I have discovered that those elements form part of the most satisfactory memories that mourners retain from the memorial service. In the loss of a young mother, I have been able to speak of lessons learned from her kindness and compassion, lessons that were learned by her children, which enabled them to say, "Mom gave us a lot to remember." A young girl's courage in the face of a disease, which she knew would take her life, provided a lesson for all of us, for which we could feel a sense of gratitude. I spoke of her courage and of Jesus' courage as he faced the cross and of God's presence with them, giving them support. Her brother said afterward, "I wondered at my sister's strength, but I guess that, with God's help, we can do a lot more than we thought." The tremendously enriching experience of becoming parents draws forth from us depths of love that can be considered part of an infant's legacy. A couple, mentioned earlier, were able because of their particular training to share a major part of the nursing care of their terminally ill infant. That opportunity provided for them an experience that they will cherish for the remainder of their lives. They have become much closer as a result of their painful experience. When one considers the fact that the loss of a child can precipitate the dissolution of a marriage, their experience is made all the more important. It is the pastor's responsibility to help make visible these elements of meaning. As he wrote about his own grief at the loss of his mother, Henri Nouwen discovered that "the deeper I entered into my own grief, the more I became aware that something new was about to be born."[22] The pastor is given the rare and priceless opportunity to help that happen for those who mourn.

TWO UNIQUELY PAINFUL EXPERIENCES

While all of the themes we have traced can bring healing to those struggling with the problem of suffering, there are two instances of loss that present issues so unique as to require their being treated separately. Infant death and suicide are two of the most painful experiences of life. They require great sensitivity in ministry to those touched by their deep anguish.

Two forms of behavior important to the pastor are frequently present in cases of infant death. When parents lose a child, they may tend to feel that it was somehow their fault. Infants are by nature helpless and require parental protection to survive. When they do not survive, many parents feel that they did not do all of the things they should have done to help their infant live. This belief is very often present in parents whose children are victims of Sudden Infant Death Syndrome (SIDS). Although research into this phenomenon indicates that it takes place despite parental love and care, nevertheless bereaved parents may carry a heavy burden of guilt.[23] It is important that those who minister be alert to this and, through supportive counseling, attempt to ease this burden. In some cases, referral to a more specialized counselor may be necessary.

Another form of behavior involved in the loss of a child is ambivalence. Mary Evans Robinson writes:

> This means that no matter how much we love someone, there are times when we feel irritated, resentful or angry toward that person. Should that person die, however, we find ourselves dwelling on the things we should or should not have done, had we known that we were to lose him.[24]

If a father's last memory before the death of his son was a moment in which the boy's disruptive behavior caused his father to discipline him, that father will likely need help to understand that, while he may feel guilty about the act of discipline and even see it as in some way contributing to his son's death, such discipline is normal. It would be helpful if parents were given an opportunity to "warm up" before the birth of their children, but such is not the case. We simply endeavor to do the best we can. A sensitive and skilled pastor will seek to focus on the good times shared between that father and his son, helping the father to see that the time he shared with his son and the warm experiences they shared together far outweigh a moment of anger. Again, more skilled therapy may be needed to ease a person through this period. A memorial sermon that lifts up the satisfying memories can help. It almost goes without saying that the pastor's regular preaching schedule should include emphasis on the need for families to take time to be together.

Finally, special attention should be paid to the father when a child dies. It has been my experience that persons instinctively seem to offer support to the mother to a much greater degree than to the father. Whether out of the mistaken notion that the father should be tough enough to handle the pain or because it is the mother who carries and gives birth to the child, it seems that fathers often do not receive enough support. A pastor who is aware of this problem can be of help to *both* parents.

All of the problems of which we have spoken, and more, are present when death comes through an act of suicide. These are some of the most difficult tragedies to test the ministry of any pastor. It is impossible in as small a space as this to do any more than just lift up a subject upon which volumes have been written. But one can touch on aspects of it that are of particular importance to the pastor.

The question that seems most often to be on the minds of the mourners has to do with whether someone who has committed suicide will "go to heaven." The question may not be expressed in exactly those terms. A parent may simply express a need to "know that my child is okay."

As near as I am able to determine, the Bible is silent on the question of suicide. Certainly, instances of it are to be found there—Saul and Judas are cases in point—but nothing is said about the meaning of the act. A careful exegesis of the sixth commandment seems to indicate that the proscription is against the act of murder, not suicide. To suggest that suicide rules an individual ineligible for the grace of God is to put oneself in the place of God, a sin about which the Bible is not at all silent.

Many questions are relevant to this discussion. William Oglesby, Jr., has noted the need for the pastor to "think through the whole notion that the prolongation of life at all times and all all costs is unambiguously a good thing. . . . Only in this generation has [come] the realization that the sustaining of life may not in every circumstance, be desirable."[25] That ethical gray areas are involved in this question there is no doubt. Pastors trained to work in a hospital setting are aware of the importance of a patient's attitude for healing. We sense that patients who decide they do not want to get better appear almost to will themselves into death. Other patients sign "living wills," requiring medical staff not to use heroic measures to prolong life if there appears to be no possibility of meaningful existence. Are these suicides? The issues are far from clear.

Much clearer is the terrible impact that is made on the lives of the survivors. Relatives are left wondering if there was something they could have done to prevent it. In the case of a youth or young adult, parents may blame themselves for not seeing the so-called "signs," which act as predictors of an attempt at suicide (the signs may never have been evident). Family members and friends are left with desires ranging from a need to express anger to a deep desire to have had an opportunity to reconcile any differences they may have had with the deceased. As the act has placed the deceased beyond the range of any of these desires, the survivors are left to struggle with their feelings.

What of the survivors? If a person has the right to take her or his life, do the survivors have rights also? What "of the right of every individual to lead an unstigmatized life, specifically, a life unstigmatized by the tabooed suicidal death of a parent, spouse, of progeny or a sibling?"[26] Indeed, it has been said that the "suicidal person places his psychological skeleton in the survivor's closet."[27] Such skeletons can remain for years.

The grief of the survivors is matched only by the load of guilt they carry, and the need for sensitive pastoral counseling may continue for a long time. Deeper therapy may even be required to help them over the guilt. Beyond the pastoral care required, the pastor's most immediate need is that of deciding how to deal with the suicide at the memorial service for the deceased.

W. A. Poovey has suggested that the pastor's best course is to "refuse to sit in judgment over anyone and to leave the deceased in the hands of a merciful and forgiving God. . . . Any statements about suicide should be left to the morning sermon or to a study group."[28]

At the same time, however, everyone who is present at the service is aware of the manner of death. It cannot simply be glossed over; several things can be helpfully said. The feelings of dismay and sorrow need to be expressed. There needs to be a strong emphasis on the good memories out of the life of the deceased, helping the survivors to see a preponderance of good over against the one act that has caused such despair. As for judging the act itself, Jesus' advice is worth remembering: "Let him who is without sin among you be the first to throw a stone" (John 8:7).

One of the occasions on which I conducted a funeral for a man who had taken his life came not long after the much-publicized suicide of the Henry Pitney Van Dusens. Remembering the first century suicide of the Jewish revolutionaries on the mountain of Masada (rather than submit to death at the hands of the Romans), William Stringfellow and Anthony Towne

> somehow associated the Van Dusen decision to die with Masada. It certainly did not seem to be a suicide to us. Perhaps, for the Van Dusens, the only way to value their own humanity in life was to die humanly by their own decision and act, instead of as victims of radical disability.[29]

There are many reasons for people behaving as they do, and none of us is so prescient as to be party to all of them. Again, the emphasis is on being nonjudgmental. What we cannot know, we should not speculate about. The sermon that stresses this, along with a strong focus on the love of God for every person, can be of great comfort to those who mourn. In the context of suicide, persons need all of the consolation the pastor can provide.

The bringing of hope and comfort to those who mourn is one of the greatest challenges facing every pastor. No doubt, there are occasions on which we might well wish that the responsibility belonged to someone else. There are services and sermons that leave us feeling empty and wrung-out, without an ounce of comfort left to give to anyone. Yet, coupled with this is also a feeling not unlike that of Paul: "Woe to me if I do not preach the gospel!" (I Cor. 9:16).

When a family's tranquility is invaded by suffering and death, the pastor is given a unique opportunity to help persons come to faith and comfort in what may be one of the most difficult periods of their lives. The pastor who accepts this responsibility in a thoughtful and sensitive manner will discover a ministry rich in love and satisfaction and marked by a profound sense of having a life used by God!

Notes

1. Nathan A. Scott, "The Burdens and Temptations of the Pulpit." In *Preaching on Suffering and a God of Love,* ed. and with a foreword by Henry J. Young (Philadelphia: Fortress Press, 1978), p. 8.

2. David Cain, "A Way of God's Theodicy: Honesty, Presence, Adventure." *The Journal of Pastoral Care* (December 1978):239.

3. Scott, "The Burdens and Temptations of the Pulpit," p. 7.

4. David H. C. Read, "The Dying Patient's Concept of God." In *Death and Ministry,* ed. J. Donald Bane et al. (New York: Seabury Press, 1977), p. 61.

5. Edgar Jackson, *When Someone Dies* (Philadelphia: Fortress Press, 1971), p. 57.

6. John B. Cobb, Jr., "The Problem of Evil and the Task of Ministry." In *Encountering Evil,* ed. Stephen T. Davis (Atlanta: John Knox Press, 1981), p. 169.

7. Jacob Philip Rudin, "Thoughts on My Wife's Death." In *But Not to Lose: A Book of Comfort for Those Bereaved,* ed. Austin H. Kutscher (New York: Frederick Fell, 1969), p. 42.

8. Edmund A. Steimle, *God, the Stranger* (Philadelphia: Fortress Press, 1979), p. 23.

9. John A. T. Robinson, *Explorations Into God* (Stanford, Calif.: Stanford University Press, 1967), p. 118.

10. Martin Marty, *A Cry of Absence* (San Francisco: Harper, 1983), p. 105.

11. William Stringfellow, *A Simplicity of Faith* (Nashville: Abingdon Press, 1982), p. 39.

12. Elisabeth Kübler-Ross, *Death: the Final Stage of Growth* (Englewood Cliffs, N.J.: Prentice-Hall, 1975), p. 164.

13. Kübler-Ross, *Questions and Answers on Death and Dying* (New York: Macmillan, 1974), p. 178.

14. In Ernest E. Bruder, *Ministering to Deeply Troubled People* (Englewood Cliffs, N.J.: Prentice-Hall, 1963), p.63.

15. Steimle, *God the Stranger*, p. 22.

16. Soelle, *Suffering*, p. 157.

17. Edgar N. Jackson, *For the Living* (Des Moines, Iowa: Channel Press, 1963), p. 78.

18. Soelle, *Suffering*, pp. 159-62.

19. Stringfellow, *A Simplicity of Faith*, p. 39.

20. Rudin, "Thoughts on My Wife's Death," p. 41.

21. Harold S. Kushner, *When Bad Things Happen to Good People* (New York: Avon Books, 1983), pp. 133-34.

22. Henri Nouwen, *In Memoriam* (Notre Dame, Ind.: Ave Maria Press, 1980), p. 59.

23. See, for example, Marilyn A. Chord and Gladys M. Scipien, "The Respiratory System." In *Comprehensive Pediatric Nursing*, ed. Gladys M. Scipien et al. (New York: McGraw-Hill, 1976), pp. 865-66.

24. Mary Evans Robinson, "When a Child Dies." In *But Not to Lose: A Book of Comfort for Those Bereaved*, ed. Austin H. Kutscher (New York: Frederick Fell, 1969), p. 108.

25. William B. Oglesby, Jr., "Care and the Suicidal Person." In *Care for the Dying*, ed. Richard N. Soulen (Atlanta: John Knox Press, 1975), pp. 16-17.

26. Edwin S. Schneidman, "To the Bereaved of a Suicide." In *But Not to Lose: A Book of Comfort for Those Bereaved*, ed. Austin H. Kutscher (New York: Frederick Fell, 1969), p. 169.

27. Ibid., p. 170.

28. W. A. Poovey, *Planning a Christian Funeral* (Minneapolis: Augsburg, 1978), p. 39.

29. Stringfellow, *A Simplicity of Faith*, p. 43.

Afterword

The problem of suffering is perhaps the most difficult of all philosophical-theological problems with which those who minister must contend. Author Alan Paton wrote that the really creative act in the face of suffering is "not to ask who dealt this wound to the creation, not to accuse God of having dealt it, but to make of one's life an instrument of God's peace."[1]

As we seek to be faithful to that task, we journey in the knowledge that there is One who has gone before us. At no other place in our ministry is the doctrine of the Resurrection more vital to us than when we confront the problem of suffering. When we come to the limits of our knowledge, when pain claims the lives of those whom we love, there is yet the voice of our Lord, reminding us that he "came that [we] might have life, and have it abundantly" (John 10:10). We are called to proclaim that gift of life in all of its fullness.

We do not limit resurrection to a period of time beyond death. While that is God's greatest gift to us—removing the sting of death—it is also present reality, available to every person who has faith in Jesus Christ. God's renewing presence can be found in persons and events that make up our day-to-day living.

> In ways that the mind cannot rationally comprehend, and only faith apprehends, he comes again to judge the living and the dead. In the communion of saints, his church, the faithful living and the faithful dead are made one. Death and resurrection—upon this fugal theme the mind of the church broods in countless ways. This message is the hinge of Christian existence, the biblical verdict on the meaning and destiny of human life.[2]

When we faithfully confront the reality of suffering and our own mortality in the light of the resurrection, we are well on our way to bringing healing to the hearts of those touched by life's inevitable pain. Perhaps our greatest need at those times is for meaning. When suffering and death claim the life of an infant or someone at the peak of life's promise, if those who grieve are to move through their time of mourning, the cause of their grief must be set into a context of meaning. In *Preaching the Story*, Edmund Steimle states this forcefully.

> What is the crying need among people today? I suspect that there are not a great many people laying awake nights tortured by the specter of an unforgiving and angry God. . . . For a lot of us the problem is not so much an angry and wrathful God, but the very real possibility that life is simply meaningless and hopeless, and that the problems we face are too overwhelming and unmanageable.[3]

It has been my experience that, when we are able to find God with us at the heart of our pain, we are given the resources that we need to hold up our heads and continue to struggle against suffering. There are, and will always be, events containing such a capacity for evil and suffering that they defy our attempts to penetrate the mystery. Paul Scherer, good pastor and preacher that he was, knew that

> When every due allowance is made . . . there is yet the unfathomable deep. What could one make of God if he could be made out. . . . There is yet the problem of evil . . . and the mystery of the good to offset it. Always somewhere the cloud and thick darkness. For those who expect it, who will not let it irritate them . . . or fill them with doubt, there is a kind of comfort in it. At least they are rid of the kind of God that the nineteenth century wanted to give the world . . . with its "fifty-seven varieties" of custom-built explanations; they may even be on the way to what the [New Testament] . . . goes about calling faith, in deep and awe-struck tones, ready to do the will of God where it is known, and to stop worrying about it where it is not.[4]

Faithfully, we do the best we can. Ultimately, we are all held in the hands of God.

Notes

1. Alan Paton, *Creative Suffering: The Ripple of Hope* (Kansas City: National Catholic Reporter Publishing Co., 1970), p. 17.

2. *A Service of Death and Resurrection,* Supplemental Worship Resource 7 (Nashville: Abingdon Press, 1979), pp. 12-13.

3. Edmund A. Steimle, Morris J. Niedenthal, and Charles L. Rice, *Preaching the Story* (Philadelphia: Fortress Press, 1980), p. 135.

4. Paul Scherer, exposition on the book of Job, in *The Interpreter's Bible,* ed. Nolan B. Harmon, vol. III (New York: Abingdon Press, 1954), pp. 1181-82.

Appendix A - Scripture Resources

For the Funeral of a Child:
   I Samuel 1:27-28—Dedicating a child to God.
   Isaiah 11:6—A little child shall lead us.
   Isaiah 40:11—The Good Shepherd.
   Matthew 18:1-4—Who is the greatest?
   Matthew 19:14—Jesus loves children.

For the Funeral of a Young Adult:
   Psalm 90:12—The value of the years.
   Matthew 11:28-30—For one who has faithfully served.
   Matthew 25—The good and faithful servant.
   John 11:25-26—The importance of faith.
   John 14:1ff—The need to trust.
   I Corinthians 15:42-58—The perishable and the imperishable body.
   Hebrews 11:13-15—For someone whose death seems without meaning.

For a Father:
   I Kings 2:1-4—A father's leadership.

Psalm 103:13—God's love and a father's love.
John 14—The father is faithful.

For a Mother:
Proverbs 31:28—Her children shall call her blessed.
Isaiah 66:13—God's comfort and a mother's comfort.
II Timothy 1:5—A mother's faith.

For Those Who Have Grown Old:
Genesis 15:15—A good old age.
Psalm 90:5-6—The naturalness of death.
Ecclesiastes 3:2—Death, a part of life.
Luke 2:29-30—A long life of faith.
II Timothy 4:6-8—Faith prepares us for dying.

For Those Who Have Suffered Through a Long Illness:
Deuteronomy 33:27—Rest from suffering.
Psalm 23—Even in pain, the Lord is present.
Romans 8:18—Suffering compared to glory.
II Corinthians 4:7-12—In pain, but not in despair.

Appendix B - Sample Sermons

The sermons that follow were all preached at the funerals or memorial services of persons whose lives had ended suddenly and prematurely. All of these deaths raised theodicy's *why* questions. All of them caused a crisis in the faith of the survivors and moved them to question God's omnipotence and goodness. All caused a significant amount of shock in the relatives closest to the deceased. They range from the death of an infant born with a rare disease to a young man who took his own life.

There are other sermons that I might have selected, but these seem to illustrate the principles, developed and offered in this volume, for preaching to those caught in the context of the problem of suffering. In each case, the identity of the person at whose funeral the sermon was delivered has been obscured, though that would not really have been necessary, as the sermons seemed to be helpful to the relatives of the deceased, and they would have been happy to have the sermons shared. It is my hope that they will also be of help to pastors and students in their preparation for preaching in this most difficult of settings.

This sermon is for Jean. She was born with a rare illness and lived six weeks before she died, much longer than the doctors predicted. Her parents were both members of a medical profession and were able to give much of the daily care that Jean required. I had never met her parents before they were referred to me by one of our church members. Her parents, feeling that death was imminent, wanted to have her baptized, but did not have a relationship with a pastor.

Jean was a beautiful child. Her death was hard for all concerned, though her parents were enabled to do much anticipatory grieving in the weeks that they cared for her with the knowledge that she could not survive her illness.

A Sermon for Jean

Text: "Let the children come to me . . . for to such belongs the kingdom of heaven." (Matthew 19:14)

There is no more difficult event in all of life than the death of a child. It violates everything that we have grown up believing to be right and just. It intrudes upon all of the hopes and dreams that we had built for our children as we awaited their coming. It leaves us feeling empty, devoid of hope.

Death, when it comes to those who are old, who have lived a long and a full life, can be accepted as a reasonable part of living. Though it hurts to lose those we love, there is yet a sense that life must be that way.

However when it comes to an infant like Jean, then we are left wondering, "If death can happen to her, then what is left? Is there anything on which we can place our trust?"

Hard on those kinds of questions are the nagging doubts that are shoved, almost brutally, into the middle of our faith. Where is God in the midst of our pain? Does God even care? Is there really any reason for believing in God, if this is all that it comes to? In the midst of our tears and our pain, we struggle to find anything that makes any sense at all.

Dick and Jane (parents), heaven knows I know how you feel, for I have been there. I know your pain. I have cried your tears. I still do. And yet, fifteen years down the road from my own son's death, I have learned some things that have been helpful for me, and I would like to share them with you.

It is common at times like this to hear people say, "Well, it's God will." Such people mean well, but I do not believe that it is God's will that any child die, any more than it was God's will that his own Son die. God's will? No, for if that is God's will, then I want nothing to do with such a God.

There are those who would say that it is from experiences such as Jean's illness and death that we are enabled to live stronger lives, that we are made better able to cope with life's troubles. Again, I believe such suggestions are offered in the hope that they will be helpful, but I find that I have more in common with Professor Dorothee Soelle, who sees in such experiences a God who may be "insensitive to human misery."[1]

What do I believe? I believe most firmly that God

hurts just as much as we do, that our faith was never given to us with a promise that we would be protected from pain, but that faith does provide us with a means of handling the pain and even of finding meaning in the midst of it. And I believe that life's meaning has very little to do with its length and very much to do with its quality. What's more, I find a basis for that belief in the faith given to us by Jesus Christ.

When the prophet Isaiah spoke of hope to an exiled nation, he said "a little child shall lead" you (11:6). When asked who would get into the kingdom of heaven, Jesus called to his side a child and said to that crowd of self-satisfied people that unless we become as children, we shall not enter the kingdom of heaven (see Matt. 18:1-5). When the disciples would have held them back, Jesus said, "Let the children come to me . . . for to such belongs the kingdom of heaven" (Matt. 19:13-14).

When God decided once and for all to show the world how he intended for people to live, he didn't do it with brass bands and banners. Rather, as preacher Paul Scherer put it, "he came down the stairs of heaven with a child in his arms."[2] Why? Because children teach us so much that older people cannot.

A young mother who lost her daughter to leukemia put it this way:

> We felt privileged to have been her parents, for she had taught us so much. I read somewhere that "suffering ceases to be suffering when it has meaning," and I feel that this is what happened inside me when I first heard that she would not be with us for long. I saw her as a teacher. . . . We are constantly reminded of the lessons that she taught us.[3]

That is exactly the way I feel about Jean. Just take a look at the gifts of learning that she shared with us.

To her grandparents: You have seen your children confront one of the most painful events of life, do battle with it, and come through it. They are hurt, yes, but they have come through it whole. If ever you had any doubts about their ability to deal with the stresses of life (and what parent does not?), then you should have no such questions now. That was Jean's gift to you.

To Dick and Jane: I would be reluctant to say that God picks certain people to be parents of children like Jean, but how fortunate she was to have had the two of you. Your training enabled you to care for her in her illness and, as you ministered to her hurt, she showed you a determination and dedication to live in a way that you will never forget. You will recognize and engender it in others.

You have experienced depths of emotion, love, and compassion given only to those who have walked through "the valley of the shadow." And you will better minister to those who come to you with hurting hearts.

You have been brought much closer to each other, as you have shared the heights and depths of each other's feelings in a way not given to all. Those are just a few of the things that Jean shared with you.

To the members of the medical staff who treated Jean: She had something for you, too. She so touched your hearts by her desire to live that you came back after work hours were done, just to sit and hold her. You shook your heads in amazement at her determination, and, in the midst of that, she helped renew your sense of the worth of what you do.

In short, we have all learned something and have become better persons for Jean's having been among us.

Questions? Oh yes, there are all kinds of them, but there is no question as to meaning. Life is never meaningless, however short it may be. Jean's life was filled with meaning and purpose.

Jesus knew that. "Let the children come unto me . . . for of such is the kingdom of heaven." He knew what a gift children are to us, and that kingdom has become his gift to Jean. Thanks be to God!

Notes

1. Dorothee Soelle, *Suffering,* trans. Everett R. Kalin (Philadelphia: Fortress Press, 1975), p. 26.

2. Paul Scherer, exposition on the book of Job, in *The Interpreter's Bible,* vol. III, ed. Nolan B. Harmon (New York: Abingdon Press, 1954), p. 1173.

3. Bernard Schoenberg et al., *Anticipatory Grief* (New York: Columbia University Press, 1974), p. 152.

The following sermon was delivered at Greg's funeral. His death, at thirteen years of age, was the result of an act of daring, for which young boys are notorious. As a result of his injuries, he was taken to a local hospital where he lingered for several days until declared clinically dead by two physicians. Though his heart continued to beat, successive electroencephalograms revealed no electrical activity in his brain.

With the physicians, I discussed with Greg's parents the possibility of donating his organs to others. This was an agonizing choice for his parents to make, since, in order for the organs to be kept infused with blood, Greg had to be taken to the operating room for organ removal while his heart was still beating.

His parents agreed to the donation. We shared a final prayer of committal at Greg's bedside, giving his care over to God. A few days later, I preached the sermon below at his memorial service. The service was attended by a group of almost two hundred students and faculty members from Greg's school as well as a contingent of medical personnel from the hospital.

A Sermon for Greg

Text: *"So it is not the will of my Father who is in heaven that one of these little ones should perish."* (Matthew 18:14)

Of all the hurts to which we are prone, I suspect that there is none that compares to the hurt we feel when we lose one of our children. When we lose someone who has come to the end of a long life, though it is painful to

141

lose anyone we love, we know that the hurt will pass in the knowledge that death is inevitable, that as Ecclesiastes reminds us, "There is a time to be born and a time to die" (3:2). We can accept it that way.

But the loss of one of our children seems to violate all the rules. We do not expect to be treated that way and, when we are, we are left with nothing but angry and painful questions.

Since we assume that God is somehow in charge of this planet, most of our questions are directed at him. Where was he when Greg needed him? Why didn't he do something? When we prayed so earnestly for Greg, why didn't God answer? But why limit our questions to Greg's death? Why is it that some very evil people live what seem to be completely untroubled lives, while those who struggle to be faithful often seem to experience nothing but trouble? There are so many questions, yet so few answers.

Biblical professor Bruce Birch spoke for most of us when he wrote, "There is something about the death of a child . . . which heightens the offense. . . . The death of a child is felt to be unacceptable . . . unnatural. . . . We [are] filled with anger and grief."[1]

All the more so with Greg, for he was all boy and "a yard wide." He was all the things that can make boys both a trial and a delight to parents. He loved to have fun, to laugh, and to show off whenever the occasion arose. Given the opportunity to be the center of attention, he never had to be asked twice. If there was a joke to be told, chances are that Greg would tell it. If there was a feat of daring to be tried, he would be first in line.

But he had his serious moments, also. The intelligence that he brought to his confirmation class and the warm memory of his considerateness on the part of those parents whose children he cared for speak to us of a boy who knew how to love. We need only to look as far as the balcony here in the church, at the large group of his classmates and teachers, to know that Greg was a boy who enjoyed the friendship of others.

But in spite of all that, Greg is gone. The place he once filled is occupied by questions and an awful, aching emptiness. That is the reality with which we must deal.

As a pastor, I am never free from wishing that I had all of the answers to all of the questions, that I could just utter the words and take away all of the hurt, for I have been where you are today. I have asked your questions and prayed your prayers. The hurt that fills your hearts today has filled mine. But I know also that there are some things that I have come to believe, and I would like to share them with you. Call it a kind of a collage, if you will, little bits and pieces of response to a puzzle, that have helped me, and I hope will help you as well.

I believe, first, that our children are not our possessions. They are, rather, a gift given to us in trust by God. As parents, we are given the responsibility to love and nurture them, to deal gently with their beautiful spirits, and to help them grow as best we are able. Not one of us is trained for the job; most of us just do the best job we know how to do. We make mistakes and, if we are big enough, we admit them and go on. We are stewards of our children's lives, and we hope to see them grow to become responsible adults. But it does not always happen, and we must pack as much living and loving into every day that their lives are meshed with ours.

And that leads to the second point of this collage today. Though a life may be short, its value is not measured in terms of how long it is, but in terms of what it gives. A rabbi, writing about the death of his young wife, said:

> The judgment of a life is not in the mathematics of the years nor in the sum of the birthdays and anniversaries. It is not saying anything important that a life is longer than another or that goodness has been rewarded if the years are many and the manner of death gentle.[2]

Life is measured in terms of what it contributes. To you, Jane [mother], the gift of warmth expressed through the hugs of a son—who would never have been caught doing that in front of his friends!—has left you with a renewed awareness of how terribly important it is that we touch and hold one another.

To you, Dick [father], the dedication of a book, which Greg said he was going to write about a subject that you both shared, tells you how much he appreciated the things that you did together and renews our awareness of how important it is that we take the time to be with our children.

To you sisters, the lightness of his jokes, his teasing, and the laughter speak of the importance of having a sense of humor.

(Here was read a letter of appreciation from the local hospital's organ donation coordinator, which stressed that Greg's life would continue to give life to others.)

These are special gifts, priceless really. Children probably give them better than anyone else, and Jesus knew that when he said that unless you become as a child, you shall not enter into the kingdom of heaven.

That brings me to the third piece of the collage. Where was God when we stood at Greg's bedside and bounced our prayers off of what seemed like silence? I'll tell you where I believe he was and is: right where he has always been, in the middle of our hurt, sharing it with us, taking it upon himself. God's heart ached as he watched his Son die. When we stood in Greg's hospital room, filled up with tears, it was God who wrapped his arms around us and said, "I know, for I have been there, too."

William Sloane Coffin, Jr., pastor of Riverside Church in New York City, lost his son recently. When that happened, he said to those who thought that it was God's will that "God's was the first of our hearts to break."[3]

Jesus said, "It is not the will of my Father who is in heaven that one of these little ones should perish" (Matt. 18:14). If God could not prevent the loss, he yet continues to give us the gift of life. Eleven disciples, scared out of their wits and hiding after Jesus' death, were somehow turned around and back out onto the street three days later to preach, daring the authorities to do whatever they wanted. Why? Because something absolutely unprecedented had happened to change all the rules. God had given life back to Jesus and through him to the disciples and to us and to Greg. "It is not the will of my Father who is in heaven that any of these little ones should perish," Jesus said. God has taken the step necessary to see that they do not. "Let the children come to me . . . for to such belongs the kingdom of God" (Mark 10:14). That is God's promise, and I believe that we can trust him to fulfill it.

Notes

1. Bruce Birch, "Biblical Faith and the Loss of Children." *The Christian Century* (October 26, 1983):965.

2. Jacob Philip Rudin, "Thoughts on My Wife's Death." In *But Not to Lose: A Book of Comfort for Those Bereaved*, ed. Austin H. Kutscher (New York: Frederick Fell, 1969), p. 41.

3. William Sloane Coffin, Jr., "Alex's Death." *In Sermons from Riverside*, a sermon preached on January 23, 1983, at New York City's Riverside Church.

The following sermon was preached at the funeral of a young man who took his own life. Don was a brilliant and sensitive person, who had much difficulty adjusting to the world's violence, particularly during the Vietnam war. Unable to find a means of coming to terms with it, he chose to leave the world that caused him so much pain. He was twenty-one years old when he died.

A Sermon for Don

Text: "These all died in faith, not having received what was promised . . . strangers and exiles on the earth." (Hebrews 11:13)

Just a few years ago, internationally known scholar, author, and former president of Union Theological Seminary, Henry Pitney Van Dusen, and his wife very quietly and deliberately one night took their lives. Their self-inflicted deaths stunned the theological world, even though Van Dusen left a letter explaining why he and his wife felt led to do what they did. They were aware that they were becoming older. They did not want to finish their remaining days in a convalescent home. They had no desire to become a burden to anyone.[1]

Some said that their deaths were terrible things to have done. Others who, while they felt badly about it, nevertheless understood why the Van Dusens had done it. To me, having read some of Van Dusen's work, one thing was evident: It is not our responsibility to judge, one way or the other, as to the rightness or wrongness of their act. There is no one of us so wise as to completely understand the motives of another person. There never will be.

I feel that way now. We will never understand what led Don to do what he did, but our's is *not* the responsibility to judge.

Saying that, however, doesn't change anything. We still know that he is gone, and the pain that goes with his passing is deep and aggravated by our inability to understand. We are, above all, profoundly aware of just how much Don had going for him.

He was a tremendously sensitive young man; he felt things at a deep level. Blessed with a mind better than that of most of us, he pursued questions until he made them yield their answers. It frustrated him that others did not see and feel as deeply as he did. His death leaves us bereft of his vision, and we are poorer.

Many of you have spoken of his drive for perfection. Whatever he put his hand to, it had to be done right, as near to perfect as he could come. But we live in an imperfect world. It frustrates all of us; it especially frustrated Don.

Don was a man whose intellect brought him straight A's in college. He was capable of good prose and poetry; he was interested in everything, especially in protecting us from ourselves. During the Vietnam war, he became a conscientious objector, but as most COs have learned, our's is not a nation that always understands such a choice. It never has been, and that, too, brought him pain.

(A poem about him, written by his family, was read here.)

Don was a man in pursuit of a world in which there is no role for pain or violence, no place for mistrust or suspicion. He looked for places and persons who would take the time to slow down and appreciate beauty and truth and compassion. He reminds me of Henry David Thoreau's vision: "If a man does not keep pace with his companions, perhaps it is because he hears a different drummer. Let him step to the music he hears, however measured or far away."[2] And step he did, as one out of step with his time, as one in search of a better world. But, like us all, he was forced to live in a world that is at times alien to our feelings. It was, perhaps, inevitable that it would bring him to despair.

I think the Bible knows of his struggle. The writer of the epistle to the Hebrews, at a moment in which he tried to deal with the death of others whose lives seemed "out of time," wrote: "These all died in faith, not having received what was promised" (11:13). He described them as "strangers and exiles on the earth."

I believe that passage was written by someone who knew and felt the sadness we share today. But it could only have been written by one who knew that the only way to handle that sadness is to rest on the God who holds our lives in the grip of his love, no matter who we are, where we go, or how we die.

He is not a God who sits far off, isolated and aloof from our pain. He is not a rock off of which our prayers rebound to us unanswered. He is One who also had a Son, and he knows our pain. He felt it before as his Son was led out and put to death.

But he is even more than that, for he is the God who gave us a promise. The writer of the epistle to the Hebrews notes that he has "prepared for us a city." It is a city that does not know the tears and suffering of this world. It is a city like unto that for which Don struggled.

For those who, like Don, love the majesty of God's creation in forest, mountain, and stream, it is now given to know the Creator of that beauty. For those who, like Don, seek answers to questions that we do not grasp, there is now given the opportunity to speak to him who is the Author of all truth. For those who, like Don, know a deep sensitivity, there is now given a companionship whose sensitivity knows no bounds.

Colonel Edwin Aldrin, the second man to walk on the moon, wrote a book titled *Return to Earth.*[3] In it he describes his bouts of depression after discovering that, having been to the moon, there were no more worlds left to conquer, or so it seemed to him. I have an idea that Don would have understood that, but we need not be concerned, for he has found the world for which he was searching. For those who are "strangers and exiles on the earth," God has prepared a city.

(At this point, a poem written and published by the deceased was read. The poem spoke of his appreciation for the beauty and variation of God's created world. It invited the listeners to join him on a metaphorical trip through that world toward our home.)

Notes

1. See, for example, William Stringfellow, *A Simplicity of Faith*, Journeys in Faith Series, ed. Robert A. Raines (Nashville: Abingdon Press, 1982), p. 43.

2. Henry D. Thoreau, *Walden and Other Writings of Henry David Thoreau*, ed. Brooks Atkinson (New York: New Modern Library, 1937), p. 290.

3. Edwin Aldrin, *Return to Earth* (New York: Random House, 1973).

Selected Bibliography

Books

Bane, J. Donald; Kutscher; Austin H.; Neale, Robert E.; and Reeves, Robert B., Jr. *Death and Ministry.* New York: Seabury Press, 1975.

Blackwood, Andrew Watterson. *The Funeral.* Philadelphia: Westminster Press, 1941.

Bowers, Margaretta K.; Jackson, Edgar N.; Knight, James A.; and LeShan, Lawrence. *Counseling the Dying.* San Francisco: Harper, 1964.

Buttrick, George A. *God, Pain, and Evil.* Nashville: Abingdon Press, 1966.

Capon, Robert Farrar. *Exit 36.* New York: Seabury Press, 1975.

————.*The Third Peacock.* Garden City, N.Y.: Doubleday, 1971.

Davis, Stephen D., ed. *Encountering Evil: Live Options In Theodicy.* Atlanta: John Knox Press, 1981.

Dillard, Annie. *Holy the Firm.* New York: Harper, 1977.

———· *Pilgrim at Tinker Creek.* New York: Bantam Books, 1974.

Ellul, Jacques. *The Ethics of Freedom.* Edited and translated by Geoffrey W. Bromiley. Grand Rapids: Mich.:Eerdman's, 1976.

Fitch, William. *God and Evil.* Grand Rapids, Mich.: Eerdman's, 1967.

Ford, D. W. Cleverly. *The Ministry of the Word.* Grand Rapids, Mich.: Eerdman's, 1979.

Fulton, Robert, ed. *Death and Iniquity.* New York: John Wiley and Sons, Inc., 1965.

Gerkin, Charles V. *Christian Experience in Modern Life.* Nashville: Abingdon Press, 1979.

Gerstenberger, Erhard S. and Schrage, Wolfgang. *Suffering.* Translated by John E. Steely. Nashville: Abingdon Press, 1980.

Gibbs, C. Earl. *Caring for the Grieving.* Corte Madera, Calif.: Omega Books, 1976.

Gill, Theodore A., ed. *To God Be the Glory.* Nashville: Abingdon Press, 1973.

Griffin, David Ray. *God, Power, and Evil: A Process Theodicy.* Philadelphia: Westminster Press, 1976.

Hebblethwaite, Brian. *Evil, Suffering, and Religion.* London: Sheldon Press, 1976.

Hick, John. *Evil and the God of Love.* San Francisco: Harper, 1978.

Horbury, William and McNeill, Brian. *Suffering and Martyrdom in the New Testament.* Cambridge: Cambridge University Press, 1981.

Howland, Elihu. *Speak Through the Earthquake*. Philadelphia: Pilgrim Press, 1972.

Hughes, Philip E. *Hope for a Despairing World*. Grand Rapids, Mich.: Baker, 1977.

Irion, Paul E. *The Funeral: Vestige or Value?* Nashville: Abingdon Press, 1966.

Jackson, Edgar N. *The Christian Funeral*. New York: Channel Press, 1966.

————. *For the Living*. Des Moines, Iowa: Channel Press, 1963.

————. *When Someone Dies*. Philadelphia: Fortress Press, 1971.

Keen, Sam. *Apology for Wonder*. New York: Harper, 1969.

————. *To a Dancing God*. New York: Harper, 1970.

Kübler-Ross, Elisabeth. *Death the Final Stage of Growth*. Englewood Cliffs, N.J.: Prentice-Hall, 1975.

————. *Questions and Answers On Death and Dying*. New York: Macmillan, 1969.

Kushner, Harold S. *When Bad Things Happen to Good People*. New York: Avon Books, 1983.

Kutscher, Austin H., ed. *But Not to Lose: A Book of Comfort for Those Bereaved*. New York: Frederick Fell, Inc., 1969.

Lewis, C. S. *The Great Divorce*. New York: Macmillan, 1946.

————. *The Problem of Pain*. New York: Macmillan, 1962.

McGill, Arthur C. *Suffering*. Foreword by Paul Ramsey and William F. May. Philadelphia: Westminster Press, 1982.

Miller, Walter M., Jr. *A Canticle for Leibowitz*. Toronto: Bantam Books, 1961.

Mills, Liston O. *Perspectives on Death*. New York: Abingdon Press, 1969.

Motter, Alton M., ed. *Preaching the Passion*. Philadelphia: Fortress Press, 1963.

Niebuhr, Reinhold. *Justice and Mercy*. Edited by Ursula M. Niebuhr. New York: Harper, 1974.

Nouwen, Henri J. M. *Creative Ministry*. Garden City, N.Y.: Doubleday and Company, 1971.

————. *In Memoriam*. Notre Dame, Ind.: Ave Maria Press, 1980.

————. *The Living Reminder*. New York: Seabury Press, 1977.

————. *The Wounded Healer*. New York: Doubleday Image Books, 1979.

Paton, Alan. "Why Suffering?" In *Creative Suffering: The Ripple of Hope*. Kansas City, Mo.: National Catholic Reporter Publishing Co., 1970.

Peck, W. Scott. *The Road Less Traveled*. New York: Simon and Schuster, 1978.

Poovey, W. A. *Planning a Christian Funeral*. Minneapolis: Augsburg, 1978.

The Interpreter's Bible, vol III. Commentary on Job, by Paul Scherer. New York: Abingdon Press, 1954.

Schilling, S. Paul. *God and Human Anguish*. Nashville: Abingdon Press, 1977.

Schoenberg, Bernard, et al. *Anticipatory Grief*. New York: Columbia University Press, 1974.

Simon, Ulrich E. *A Theology of Auschwitz*. London: Victor Gollancz, 1967.

Sockman, Ralph W. *The Meaning of Suffering*. New York: Abingdon Press, 1961.

Soelle, Dorothee. *Suffering*. Translated by Everett Kalin. Philadelphia: Fortress Press, 1975.

Sontag, Frederick. *God, Why Did You Do That?* Philadelphia: Westminster Press, 1970.

Soulen, Richard N., ed. *Care for the Dying.* Atlanta: John Knox Press, 1975.

Steimle, Edmund A. *God, the Stranger.* Philadelphia: Fortress Press, 1979.

Stewart, James S. *The Strong Name.* New York: Charles Scribner's Sons, 1941.

Stone, Howard W. *Crisis Counseling.* Philadelphia: Fortress Press, 1976.

Stringfellow, William. *A Simplicity of Faith.* Journeys of Faith series, edited by Robert A. Raines. Nashville: Abingdon Press, 1982.

Sweazey, George E. *Preaching the Good News.* Englewood Cliffs, N.J.: Prentice-Hall, Inc., 1976.

Switzer, David K. *The Minister as Crisis Counselor.* Nashville: Abingdon Press, 1974.

Thielicke, Helmut. *Living With Death.* Translated by Geoffrey W. Bromiley. Grand Rapids, Mich.: Eerdman's, 1983.

Towner, W. Sibley. *How God Deals With Evil.* Philadelphia: Westminster Press, 1976.

Updike, John. *A Month of Sundays.* Greenwich, Conn.: Fawcett Publications, Inc., 1974.

Urban, Linwood and Walton, Douglas N. *The Power of God.* New York: Oxford University Press, 1978.

Vanauken, Sheldon. *A Severe Mercy.* London: Hodder and Stoughton, 1970.

Viets, Wallace T. *My God, Why?* Nashville: Abingdon Press, 1966.

Weatherhead, Leslie D. *When the Lamp Flickers.* New York: Abingdon-Cokesbury Press, 1948.

―――. *Why Do Men Suffer?* New York: Abingdon Press, 1936.

―――. *The Will of God.* Nashville: Abingdon Press, 1972.

Wenham, John S. *The Goodness of God.* Downers Grove, Ill.: Inter-Varsity Press, 1974.

Wiesel, Elie. *Five Biblical Portraits.* South Bend, Ind.: Notre Dame Press, 1981.

―――. *Messengers of God.* New York: Random House, 1976.

―――. *Night.* Foreword by François Mauriac. Translated by Stella Rodway. New York: Avon Books, 1960.

―――. *The Trial of God.* Translated by Marion Wiesel. New York: Random House, 1979.

Young, Henry J., ed. *Preaching on Suffering and a God of Love.* Foreword by Nathan A. Scott, Jr. Philadelphia: Fortress Press, 1978.

Articles

Birch, Bruce C. "Biblical Faith and the Loss of Children." *The Christian Century* (October 26, 1983): 965-67.

Brown, Robert McAfee. "Starting Over: New Beginning Points for Theology." *The Christian Century* (May 14, 1980):545-49.

Cain, David. "A Way of God's Theodicy: Honesty, Presence, Adventure." *The Journal of Pastoral Care* (December 1978):239-50.

Coffin, William Sloane, Jr. *"Alex's Death."* Sermon preached at Riverside Church, New York City, on January 23, 1983.

Dedmon, Robert. "Job as Holocaust Survivor." *The St. Luke's Journal of Theology* (June 1983):165-85.

Durham, Ronald O. "Evil and God: Has Process Made Good on Its Promise?" *Christianity Today* (June 2, 1978):10-14.

Fackre, Gabriel. "Narrative Theology." *Interpretation* (October 1983):340-52.

Kaufman, Peter I. "Daniel Day Williams and the Science of Suffering." *Union Seminary Quarterly Review* (Fall 1978):35-46.

McWilliams, Warren. "Daniel Day Williams' Vulnerable and Invulnerable God." *Encounter* (Winter 1983): 73-89.

Weborg, John. "Abraham Joshua Heschel: A Study in Anthropodicy." *The Anglical Theological Review* (October 1979):483-97.

Weinberg, Werner. "A Dutch Couple." *The Christian Century* (June 22-19, 1983):611-15.

Index of Scripture References

Genesis
22.................................... 71

Exodus
20:13................................ 122

Numbers
6:25-26............................. 94

II Samuel
12:16-17............................ 87

Job
1:5.................................... 30
1:8.................................... 28
1:11.................................. 39
1:18.................................. 31
13:15................................. 36

Psalms
90:12................................. 112
137:4................................. 113

Ecclesiastes
3:1a................................... 108
3:2a........................... 25, 108

Isaiah
41:1................................... 109
49:4.................................. 71
50:6.................................. 71
53:3-12............................. 71
53:4.................................. 72

Jeremiah
27:17................................ 33

Amos
3:2.................................... 46

Matthew
5:45........................... 21, 70
6:34.................................. 111

16:24-25............................ 115
28:20................................ 74

Luke
22:44................................ 71

John
5:17.................................. 70
8:7.................................... 124
9:2.................................... 46
10:10................................ 128
11:35................................ 71
14:18................................ 110

Romans
3:23.................................. 51
5:3-4................................. 71
8:18.................................. 107
8:21-22........................ 65, 70
8:28........................... 38, 107

I Corinthians
9:16.................................. 125
15.................................... 101
15:46b............................... 99

II Corinthians
2:9.................................... 54
12:7.................................. 38
12:9.................................. 65

Hebrews
11:39-40............................ 68
12:7.................................. 52

James
1:2-5................................. 71

I Peter
3:15.................................. 84

Revelation
20.................................... 40

Index of Authors

Augustine, Bishop of Hippo, 23, 49

Bonhoeffer, Dietrich, 75
Buechner, Frederick, 84
Buttrick, George A., 26, 27, 42, 48-49

Cain, David, 21n.2, 85, 126n.2
Capon, Robert Farrar, 36, 60, 79
Cobb, John B., Jr., 34n.4, 105
Coffin, William Sloane, 69

Davis, Stephen, 50
DeArment, Daniel C. 92
Dedmon, Robert, 35n.17
Dillard, Annie, 24, 26-27, 45, 61
Durham, Ronald O., 72

Ellul, Jacques, 90

Fackre, Gabriel, 65
Fisher, Wallace, 47
Ford, D. W. Cleverly, 85

Griffin, David Ray, 63, 66-67

Hammarskjöld, Dag, 14
Heller, Joseph, 47
Hick, John, 65-67

Irion, Paul E., 22

Jackson, Edgar, 105, 115

Kaufman, Peter I., 36
Keen, Sam, 21
Kübler-Ross, Elisabeth, 99, 112-13
Kushner, Harold S., 31, 117

Lewis, C. S., 52-53, 55

McGill, Arthur C., 41
McGregor, Geddes, 51, 62
MacLeish, Archibald, 16, 19, 24-25, 38, 48

Marty, Martin, 72, 109
Miller, Walter M., Jr., 50
Moltmann, Jürgen, 69

Neibuhr, Reinhold, 20
Nouwen, Henri J. M., 30, 70, 88, 90, 96, 119

Oglesby, William, Jr., 122

Paton, Alan, 43, 68, 128
Peck, M. Scott, 82
Plantinga, Alvin, 50, 51
Poovey, W. A., 123
Pruyser, Paul, 91

Read, David H. C., 104
Robinson, John A. T., 55
Robinson, Mary Evans, 120
Roth, John K., 59, 65, 82
Rudin, Jacob Philip, 106

Scherer, Paul, 33, 39-40, 130
Schilling, S. Paul, 26, 39, 51, 66
Schneidman, Edwin S., 123
Scott, Nathan, 103
Sockman, Ralph, 44, 54
Soelle, Dorothee, 19, 28, 31-32, 48, 54-55, 70, 84, 114, 115
Sontag, Frederick, 51
Steimle, Edmund A., 27, 28, 114, 129
Stewart, James S., 23
Stringfellow, William, 72, 110, 115, 124

Tillich, Paul, 62

Vanauken, Sheldon, 45-46, 53

Weatherhead, Leslie D., 66
Weinberg, Warner, 75
Wiesel, Elie, 27, 33, 85, 99
Williams, Daniel Day, 64